on

18
0 s

by A. Rey Pamatmat

1.

A good ten-minute play is the ultimate **playwright** flex.

It says, "I can give you a full meal before these other plays have even started cook-ing! What...? You want more? NOT TODAY!"

A good ten-minute can keep your attention with mundane conversation about toddlers

or make you **laugh about** someone's **dad dying**

or convince you that the **grotesque** murder of a child is the sensible conclusion to a problem.

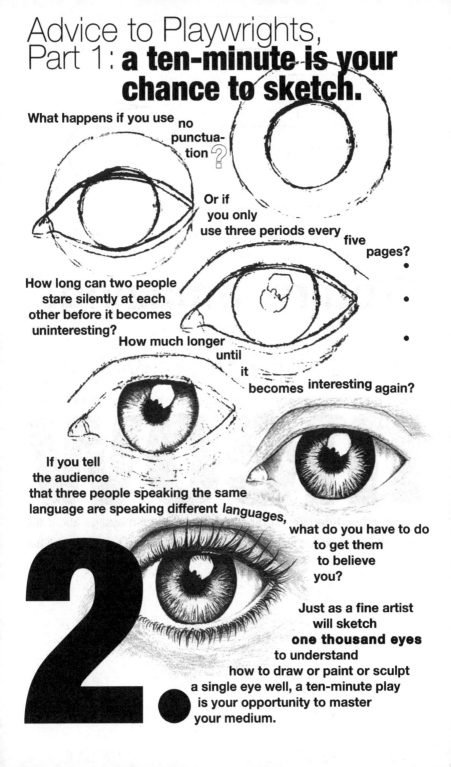

Advice to Playwrights,
Part 1: a ten-minute is your chance to sketch.

What happens if you use no punctua-tion?

Or if you only use three periods every five pages?

How long can two people stare silently at each other before it becomes uninteresting?

How much longer until it becomes interesting again?

If you tell the audience that three people speaking the same language are speaking different languages, what do you have to do to get them to believe you?

Just as a fine artist will sketch **one thousand eyes** to understand how to draw or paint or sculpt a single eye well, a ten-minute play is your opportunity to master your medium.

2.

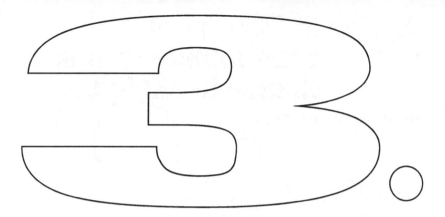

3.

One of my favorite ten-minute plays is *You're Amazing* by Leah Nanako Winkler. One of its pages contains two people who just say,

"You're amazing,"

to   each   other.

FOR A FULL PAGE.

And then, on another half page, two murderers just

meow

at each other. I don't even buy the play's cynical message about the impossibility of young love, but I don't care because Leah uses all her

playwright powers
to make you watch

,   and   you   do,

and   you   love   doing   it.

4.

There are some people

who hate the entire concept

of **reading** or **seeing** ten-minute plays.

If this is you,

just

shut up

, be patient,

and read or see some.

If you don't like one,

it will be over soon

and there will be an opportunity

to like the next one soon. →

5.

There are some people who hate the entire concept of *writing* ten-minute plays.
If you're a playwright who doesn't need to sketch, you have an excess of confidence
and probably won't be a playwright for very long. It isn't a vocation that will fuel
or satisfy such steady self-assuredness.

Advice to The Audience:

6. if you like reading
a ten-minute play —
or any play, really —
get some other
humans together
and read it out loud.
You're welcome.

Once I told my agent that I wanted to be Thornton Wilder and write experimental short plays and one-acts for the rest of my life. But I wanted them all to get produced, and I still wanted to make enough money to survive. She very encouragingly said, "Great! First step, write *Our Town.*" I stopped pursuing this line, but I imagine step two would have been, "Write *The Skin of Our Teeth.*"

8.

Advice to Playwrights, Part 2:
if you can't keep an audience interested for ten minutes, you won't be able to keep them in it for ninety minutes or two hours or for your five-play cycle. **So whip out your pens or phones** (or whatever you write with these days) **and GET**

FLEXING

PUNCH people in the Face

with your brilliance.
Make them WTF
in less time than it takes to think,

"WTF!"

Manipulate them into **laughs**, **tears**, and **panic attacks**. Remind them in mere moments how much they once **loved** what they **lost**, coveted what they now have, and are simultaneously filled with **gratitude** and **regret** about all of it.

Not everything
in the world
needs to be per-
fect to be good.
Some ten-min-
ute plays are a
mess, and that's
the entire rea-
son they work.

9.

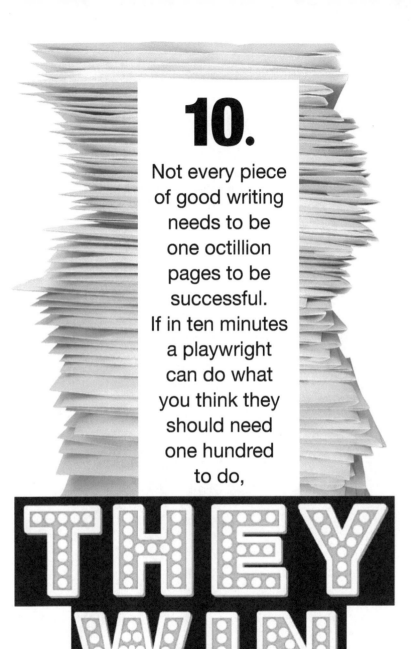

10.

Not every piece of good writing needs to be one octillion pages to be successful. If in ten minutes a playwright can do what you think they should need one hundred to do,

THEY WIN

man·i·fes·to (man-*uh*-**fes**-to) A public declaration of principles, policies, or intentions, especially of a political nature.

edited by
A. Rey Pamatmat

Volume 6

Suzanne Bailie

Kelleen Conway Blanchard

Anuhea Brown

Brian Dang

Bret Fetzer

Mikki Gillette

Ki Gottberg

Emily Haver

Maggie Lee

Barbara Lindsay

Willow McLaughlin

July Monday

Beth Raas-Bergquist

Wayne Rawley

Matt Smith

Ozzy Wagner

Matthew Weaver

Ky Weeks

Michael Yichao

CONTENTS

ACKNOWLEDGMENTS

Rain City Projects wishes to thank the following for their assistance in compiling this volume: Meghan Arnette, Becky Bruhn, Andrew Lee Creech, Bret Fetzer, May Nguyen Lee, Darian Lindle, K. Brian Neel, Kristina Sutherland Rowell, and Matt Smith.

Rain City Projects is powered by Shunpike, a 501(c)(3) non-profit agency that provides independent arts groups in Washington State with services, resources, and fiscal sponsorship. Rain City Projects is also sponsored in part by 4Culture.

FOREWORD

As Rain City Projects moves into our thirty-second year of existence, we decided to mix things up and pay homage to something that the playwrights of the Pacific Northwest create in abundance and with great skill: the ten-minute play!

First, a bit of foundational information: Rain City Projects, a.k.a. RCP, is a Seattle-based organization dedicated to supporting and promoting professional playwrights and their work. We do this by holding events that build community, introduce playwrights to directors, and provide space and time for writing. Every few years, we also publish a new book of plays in our Manifesto series, edited by a nationally-known playwright. The past five volumes highlighted full-length or longer one-act plays from playwrights with a connection to the Pacific Northwest. But this time around, we wanted to celebrate the magic and versatility of the ten-minute play. The Pacific Northwest has a rich history of festivals that highlight the ten-minute play: 14/48: The World's Quickest Theater Festival, Live Girls! Theater's Quickies Festival, Island Theatre's Ten-Minute Play Festival, and many more. So we sent out the call for plays and wow, did our inbox get exciting!

We approached renowned playwright A. Rey Pamatmat to edit this volume. He said, "Yes!" and we did a happy dance. We knew the number of submissions would be high so we gathered a group of theatre artists to be readers. Each play was read anonymously, without author names, by two different readers (readers did not evaluate their own plays) and was given a numerical score based on a rubric. The plays with the highest average score moved on to the next round to be considered by our editor. We had so many wonderful submissions, in a wide variety of styles and topics. But as we have stated in the past: "The Manifesto Series is not a 'greatest hits' anthology—each editor has an ax to grind, a chip on the shoulder, a vision of how theater would be better if only it had more of THIS. Each editor looks over the body of work written and produced in the Pacific Northwest and chooses plays that embody, articulate, or make manifest that editor's particular THIS." Rey then selected the plays for this book based on his manifesto, his own particular THIS.

Once completed, this book will be sent to theatre companies and universities across the United States. It is our hope that, among other things, a teacher finds exactly what they need for their class, a group of drama students find the right play that makes them shine, and that a theatre company, planning a night of shorts, finds most of them right here in this book.

Enjoy!

—Anuhea Brown, Kate Danley, Monika Elmont, Maggie Lee, and Juliet Waller
Rain City Projects Board Members

SUZANNE BAILIE is an award-winning playwright and artist. Suzanne wrote her first play while working on a coffee farm in the jungles of Hawaii. Her short play was produced by a local theatre company and she hasn't stopped hitting the keyboard since. Suzanne's full-length play, *Hardened Criminals*, was the recent winner of the Bill and Peggy Hunt Playwright Festival. Her short plays and monologues have been produced across the United States and internationally. Her published short plays include: *The Raspberry*, *Baby Jesus Does Not Kill Ninja Zombies*, *Mel and Mona*, *Fish Queen*, and *The Blankie*. Her stage works are bold reality that merge uncomfortable truth and unexpected laughter. Besides writing her favorite activities are drinking strong coffee, creating collages, oil painting, and travel.

Suzanne Bailie

Joie De Vivre

CHARACTERS:

TRACY   Gender neutral. Enthusiastic and a persistent
                       salesperson.

NOVA   Female. Kind-hearted. Partnered with DEAN.
                       Looks middle age but is 250 years old.

DEAN   Male. Ready for a change. Partnered with
                       NOVA. Looks middle age but is 205 years old.

SETTING:

A bare stage, which serves as the viewing area for the potential purchase
of a Sprout.

As lights rise, NOVA and DEAN stand looking at the audience. They are both charmed by what they observe.

NOVA: They are so precious. So much cuteness in something so small. They're very mobile.

DEAN: (*jumps in enthusiasm*) Look at that one. It is just jumping. Isn't jumping spectacular?

NOVA: What are they doing now? Adorable.

DEAN: Look, they're turning in circles then they fall over. What a silly thing to do.

NOVA: Is that, laughing? They are laughing while they turn.

DEAN: We'd be making barfing noises if we twirled until we flopped over.

NOVA: Laughter is good, right?

DEAN: Most definitely.

TRACY enters

TRACY: Don't you love that energy? I'm Tracy your zeal specialist. It is a pleasure to meet you. Dean and Nova, correct?

DEAN: Yes. We're excited to be here.

TRACY: I'm excited to close this deal and bring you new joy. I'm known as the best of the zest. Get it? Zest for life, I'm the best.

NOVA: Zesty congratulations Tracy. These Sprouts seem to vibrate they're so alive. Do they ever sleep?

DEAN: Like batteries endless energy.

TRACY: Our Sprouts sleep deep. A result of playful exhaustion and having their little backs rubbed every night while care-takers sing lullabies.

NOVA: What are they two, three?

TRACY: You have an astute eye Nova. These Sprouts are the optimal age. We never have any past four. If, on the *odd chance* that does occur they are used in other ways.

DEAN: I thought the legal cut off was five.

TRACY: At Home Grown we pride ourselves on purity and efficacy of our product. Research shows when primary teeth fail, the Sprouts wonderment quotient decreases. Can't have that can we?!

NOVA: I hardly remember losing teeth, that was so long ago. It must be painful, how horrible we went through that.

DEAN: I can't recall the last time I felt any pain. I think one bleeds from their gums when they lose a tooth.

TRACY: Very perceptive Dean. As short as a hundred years ago losing blood led to frailty, disfigurement, even death.

DEAN: I had a frail grandma. You know before we had our aging options. She walked with a cane, had broke her hip or something I think, no teeth, grey hair even.

NOVA: With no teeth how did she eat? Was she terribly unattractive?

DEAN: I remember her skin was soft and wrinkly. You could see the blue veins in her hands. She placed, something, in her mouth, like they were fake teeth.

NOVA: Poor thing.

TRACY: Dentures.

DEAN: At night she put them in a glass of water by her bed. Creepy.

NOVA: Thank goodness our teeth never rot.

TRACY: And stay as white as Elmer's glue.

DEAN: (*points at someone in audience*) I like that one. Watch it kick that red ball, chase it down and do it again. Go Sprout Go!

TRACY: Total vitality. Outstanding exultation of spirit cultivated right here at Home Grown.

DEAN: That's the one for me.

TRACY: You have an eye for quality. How about you Nova?

NOVA: (*pauses*) I'm sorry Tracy it, maybe, I'm not sure if I'm ready.

DEAN: Again!?

NOVA: It is just I don't—

DEAN: Come on Nova! I am not going to Canada and deal with that paperwork. This place has a solid record every crop certified organic and no genetic markers for depression, moodiness and all that other unpleasant stuff.

TRACY: We guarantee curiosity, humor, optimism, and wonderment.

DEAN: Trust me, you need wonderment Nova. Look at those Sprouts. You are witnessing untainted joy, innocence. What is wrong with you? How can you not want this?

NOVA: Nothing is wrong with me. The last couple of times you came home and said, "here" take this pill. This, this is different.

DEAN: The old synthetic stuff is replaced with Sprouts. (*motions toward the audience*) It's the best thing ever.

TRACY: Our ancestors ate fresh food grown in fertilized soil, exposed to the sun's rays and watered by rain. Here, at Home Grown, that same science is applied to nurture those "essential" ingredients in the Sprouts.

DEAN: You know, Ian told me Patricia refused to do this. Ian says he's living with a ninety-year-old from way back. Patricia only wants to hook up to her V.R. and get lost. Another two-hundred-year-old zombie.

NOVA: That was *her* choice to make.

TRACY: So sad, losing one's zest. Especially since science has created a non-ending supply of cheerful enjoyment.

DEAN: Nova I'm serious. You don't want me to find someone else . . . or force me to.

NOVA: What?! If I don't? Then . . . are you saying? You're doing this here. Now!?

DEAN: I won't live with someone like Patricia. It is revolting.

NOVA: You're revolting.

TRACY: We have excellent financing if necessary.

NOVA: Your ultimatum is revolting especially here in front of our, our wonderment dealer! (*to Tracy*) Nothing personal Tracy. (*to Dean*) You are so disgustingly self-absorbed.

DEAN: Yes, I am. Everyone living like we do are disgustingly self-absorbed. I am too old to act like my wants and needs are not important. If my seat is too hard, I ask for a cushion. Drink not cold enough I ask for ice. This is no different than making my life more comfortable.

NOVA: Too old? You are barely two-hundred. But you're acting like a spoiled baby.

TRACY: (*to Dean*) You converted at the optimum age. Amazing skin tone and muscle to fat ratio. And you Nova, goodness, you are holding up excellently.

NOVA: (*uncomfortable*) Uh, thanks for noticing.

TRACY: Let me focus on, your, concerns Nova.

NOVA: Well, is this authentic? Are these Sprouts truly happy? How do I know this isn't the result of a stimulant given in their morning feeding?

TRACY: We recommend a facility tour where you can witness embryos expertly lab created. You can also virtually visit their playroom, dining area and sleeping quarters to monitor activities

NOVA: We all know virtual is extremely malleable.

TRACY: Tight quality control of our inventory allows bonding only between one Sprout and one hand selected care-taker. So only virtual allowed. Have you two decided what form of payment works best for your budget?

DEAN: You agreed to this. No more putting it off.

NOVA: Shut up Dean I know what I said. Have you forgotten your needs are not my responsibility or priority?

DEAN: You will appreciate it. Everyone says it is the best. Ian can't stop raving about it.

TRACY: Documentation shows your previous supplements used fade to nothing after fifty years. Your paperwork indicates that was sixty years ago. Gosh, you know what that means? A decade of (*shows sad face and sad body*). Am I right?

DEAN: When was the last time you felt anything Nova? Anything good? We barely make it to early happy hours on most days.

NOVA: They are so endearing, you know, sweet. I don't know, it seems like . . . (*beat*) We went to an agency in Asia.

TRACY: Oh dear.

NOVA: Their versions of these Sprouts were thin. I worried they didn't have enough food, maybe even went to bed hungry. They seemed more, mature, even intelligent, for their age.

TRACY: I am so sorry you experienced those uncomfortable feeling. We completely forbid encouraging the intellectual part of the Sprout's brain.

NOVA: Could you imagine if they knew?

TRACY: We do offer an incentive if customers pay with cash.

NOVA: So pretty. Their cheeks. They look so soft.

DEAN: Looks make no difference. It is that, little area, in the brain we are after. All that cuteness is juiced up and turned into regenerating goo. You know they are not real toddlers.

TRACY: Heaven to Betsy! That's not true. They are one-hundred percent real humans. Clones do not have the necessary bits to be effective for our needs. Here at Home Grown our primary goal is fill our human Sprouts with joy joy joy during their few short years.

NOVA: That blond one, look, she is playing with a puppy now.

TRACY: We provide our Sprouts new experiences to stimulate their dentate gyrus, that's where curiosity comes from.

DEAN: I am all in. The one that kicks the ball. That's mine.

TRACY: Astute choice, number 4740. Unfortunately, if any Sprouts are not used for the reason for their creation, they will be parted out for organ harvesting. Not a happy time for them.

NOVA: Fine. That little one does seem very happy, curious.

TRACY: It is good for the environment, no resources wasted.

DEAN: Waste not want not, and then, want more get more.

NOVA: Fine.

TRACY: Outstanding. Shall we write up your contract?

DEAN: I heard we can request our own favorite flavors.

TRACY: Certainly. Pineapple, tutti fruitti, chocolate? Or mix and match.

DEAN: How about milk and honey, because that is sort of what this is. Our lost land of milk and honey.

TRACY: Very poetic. Nova?

NOVA: Flavor? I don't care. Whatever.

DEAN: Ian is leaving Patricia. She won't even notice.

NOVA: Stop insinuating I am like Patricia.

TRACY: Okay. You seem drawn to that 4736 model. If we write this up today the extraction can be done tonight and your sweet chewy life enhancing candy will be delivered tomorrow.

> *DEAN and TRACY start to head off stage. NOVA hesitates looking at audience.*

DEAN: Come on love, let's experience a life that feels worth living again. A rebirth.

TRACY: You will both be over the moon with your new enthusiastic joie de vivre. Remember me fifty years from now. Shall we go fill out the paperwork?

NOVA: Do the Sprouts feel it? It doesn't hurt, right?

TRACY: Like it states in the brochure and true for all of us: Only pleasant experiences are allowed in the Sprouts' enchanted lives and our very very long ones.

All start to exit.

DEAN: You are making me so happy dear.

NOVA: Dean, be a dear and please shut the hell up.

KELLEEN CONWAY BLANCHARD is a Seattle-based playwright that focuses on the monstrous and mysterious with funny, female centered plays. Her work has been seen/produced at Annex Theatre, Macha Monkey, Balagan Theatre, Live Girls!, 18th and Union, Weird and Awesome, 12 Minutes Max, 14/48, Seattle Public Theater, and FringeACT. Outside of Seattle, her plays have been seen at Strand Theater Company and The Players Theater with Spit and Vigor and been part of Eight Tens at Eight in Santa Cruz, the 2nd Annual Festival of New Short Plays in Belfast, Maine, and Perishable Theatre's Women's Playwriting Festival.

Kelleen Conway Blanchard

Daddy

CHARACTERS:

BOBBY	The brother. A young man home from military school
GENEVIEVE	The oldest sister. Sickly.
CLARISSA	The youngest sister. Deeply creepy— has a headless doll.
MOTHER	A rather dim little girl of a woman
NARRATOR	On the mike
A MOSTLY HEADLESS DOLL	Voiced by the Narrator
STONER	Voiced by the Narrator

SETTING:

The living room of a lovely family.

The Narrator stands aside—on the mike.

NARRATOR: Once upon a time, there was a lovely family, inside and out. Sturdy as a luxury liner. At the helm steering their proud ship was Daddy. Daddy, a man like a wedge of cheese. A man of jowl and principle.

BOBBY: And that's when we found him eaten by the dog.

MOTHER: (*Screams*)

GENEVIEVE: You should not have said that Bobby.

BOBBY: It's true though, isn't it? Dead on the john Momma and his ears chewed clean off.

MOTHER: (*Screams*)

GENEVIEVE: A mature person would have said, "We regret that daddy has passed." A mature adult type person would have left out the disgusting details.

MOTHER: (*Sobs and Screams*)

GENEVIEVE: Now Mother, now. Daddy's spirit lives on here. In all of us.

CLARISSA: Like a possession. A haunting. We'll drag his spirit with us like a boulder nailed to our backs.

MOTHER: He loved that dog. He kissed that dog on the mouth.

BOBBY: I could've said ingested by his dog.

MOTHER: (*Hiccuppy sobs*)

BOBBY: Biscuit's a good dog.

GENEVIEVE: Shut up. Shut up. I don't want to remember Daddy that way. I want to think about him when he still had his hands and all of his nose.

BOBBY: I want to talk at the funereal.

GENEVIEVE: I think you have proved yourself too much of a child. Too unable to swallow the bad and spit back out good.

BOBBY: Don't you call me no names. I'll call you a couple of names.

GENEVIEVE: I will do the speaking because I have the self control. I will say, "He was an American citizen of this country."

CLARISSA: He toiled. He liked meat boiled. He kept his hinges oiled.

MOTHER: He is gone. What will we do I wonder? He was always here. And now he won't be. It will be as though something is missing.

The dog starts barking. The Narrator can do this sound effect.

GENEVIEVE: Shut that dog up. For Christ's sake.

BOBBY: Aww Biscuit just wants to say howdy. He's lonely as hell. He was holed up in that bathroom for four days until we found them. He's got some shit to get off his chest.

GENEVIEVE: I'm gonna put that dog down.

BOBBY: You try it. I'll stab you in the stomach, take you all day to bleed to death. (*He pulls out a switchblade and approaches menacingly*) Come on. Make your move.

GENEVIEVE: Mother he's going to kill me. He's got a weapon.

MOTHER: Children. Gather. Put down your knife honey. Your father knew this day would come. He knew that life was a finite gift but that the love in families is eternal. So, he prepared for this day—Here is something he wanted you each to have.

She hands each of them a box. They all open them to reveal identical cross pens.

CLARISSA: (*Puts hers down the doll's neck*)

BOBBY: (*Whistles and throws his for the dog*)

GENEVIEVE: Thank you. (*puts hers behind her ear. Turns to Bobby*) Daddy never felt you measured up, you know.

BOBBY: That's ass.

GENEVIEVE: He didn't.

BOBBY: Well he gave me that fuck ass pen. Didn't he? Proves something.

GENEVIEVE: Watch your mouth. Have some respect for the dead. Some of us loved him, right Clarissa?

CLARISSA: (*To her headless doll*) And in the dark the monsters crawl. They crawl like water. They eat nothing but fingers while you sleep. They slide into your blankets. You don't hear them coming. They are silent and when you wake up, as the windows open, you look down and your hands are bloody paws. You have to get hooks for your hands and a patch and a parrot. The monsters, they turn you into a pirate, send you to the sea.

BOBBY: Where's its head ?

CLARISSA: It's not an it. It's a she. Her name is Beatrice. She has feelings.

BOBBY: Where's her head?

CLARISSA: That's how she came. She doesn't need it.

BOBBY: Everybody needs a head. How does she eat?

CLARISSA: She sucks it in through her neck.

BOBBY: Show me.

CLARISSA: It's private.

GENEVIEVE: Clarissa you are almost a grown person. You are too old to have a doll.

CLARISSA: Just because you don't think she's alive, doesn't mean she isn't alive. She lives. At night.

BOBBY: Leave her alone Genevieve.

GENEVIEVE: Don't talk to me. Criminal. You all make me sick. I feel sick. I'm getting a giant hive. All of you are giving me a hive.

CLARISSA: You smell like spit.

GENEVIEVE: Mother.

MOTHER: I think we should have a moment of silence for Daddy.

NARRATOR: For a moment everyone remembers Daddy. Bobby remembers Daddy

The lights shift to Bobby. The Narrator become's Bobby's stoner friend.

NARRATOR: (*As stoner friend*) You can't mix that shit man, I'm telling you.

BOBBY: This bong can purify. It's the bong of the gods. Baptize me.

NARRATOR/STONER: Suck it. You have to really hold it.

BOBBY: I feel like puking, I'm gonna puke big.

NARRATOR/STONER: I told you not to mix in all that paint thinner man. You do that shit after.

BOBBY: Shut up. Fuck. Fuck. Do you hear something? It's my fucking father. Do I look stoned? Do I? Do I? Do I? Do I look stoned? Look at me. Look at me. Fuck. Fuck. I look stoned. Oh fuck. I look totally stoned. Look at my head man. My head is huge. He will know. He will totally know. Jesus Christ. He'll send me to that fucking military academy. Okay. Okay. Now do I look stoned? Look at me. Fuck. I look okay right? If I turn sideways I look fine.

The lights shift to Genevieve.

NARRATOR: Genevieve remembers Daddy

Throughout the NARRATOR makes harrumphing sounds and rustles his newspaper—as Daddy.

GENEVIEVE: I hurt myself in gym class. On the tether ball net. I think there is a dent in my eye. So, the nurse said I could come home. Because, I'm allergic to the smell of the tumbling mats. They make my ear bleed. And then, I could have those fits again. And you said Daddy. You said, if I have the fits again you're taking me out of school because, that's not good for people to be seeing. My fits are private. Right? Right? Do you want to see where I got bit by this boy during study hall? I had to have a shot for that. Daddy? Daddy? Do you want me to get you a martini? Dry with three olives? Daddy?

The lights shift to Mother.

NARRATOR: Mother remembers Daddy.

Mother eating chocolates messily from a box.

MOTHER: At night he's so quick, like a jack rabbit. I think it's nice that he just gets it done. He doesn't muck around with alot of wet stuff like in those silly movies. He's efficient. Sometimes I don't even notice. I go right on eating chocolates or reading my ladies home journal and boom he's all done. Zipped up and asleep. He makes noises like a kitten while he sleeps. It hurts my ears. So, a lot of times while he's sleeping I'll pinch him hard under the armpit. Pinch and twist. And he'll stop making those noises. We've been married for thirty seven years. I always said I'd marry a man named Harold and I just went right ahead and did.

The lights shift to Clarissa.

NARRATOR: Clarissa remembers Daddy

The Narrator speaks as Clarissa's Doll.

NARRATOR/THE DOLL: Daddy eats too much. What if he eats everything and there's nothing left for us? I don't like that Daddy. I wish we could get a new Daddy. I wish we could get a smaller Daddy who would not get mashed potatoes in his mustache. I wish we could get a Daddy that did not unbuckle his pants after dinner. I wish we could find a Daddy that would buy us all of the hamsters we need.

CLARISSA: The hamsters never last.

NARRATOR/THE DOLL: Hamsters and snakes can be mated.

CLARISSA: I think they can.

NARRATOR/THE DOLL: I wonder how we could get a new Daddy?

CLARISSA: Well, we'd have to get rid of the old one first.

NARRATOR/THE DOLL: We would. Wouldn't we?

The action returns to normal. General lighting returns.

GENEVIEVE: Mother?

MOTHER: Hmm?

GENEVIEVE: How come you didn't notice Daddy was in the bathroom all that time?

MOTHER: I don't know honey. He was like that. Sometimes we'd be in the same room for hours and I'd plumb forget he was there. Then, he'd snort and spit in that hankerchief and I'd think, "Oh yeah. There he is."

NARRATOR: Once upon a time there was a lovely family, inside and out. Sturdy as a luxury liner. At the helm steering their proud ship was Daddy. Daddy a man like a wedge of cheese. A man of jowl and principle.

Lights fade.

ANUHEA BROWN (*Aw-new-hay-uh*) is an emerging playwright based in New York, New York. She is a proud Graduate of New York University with a Master's Degree in Dramatic Writing from the Rita and Burton Goldberg Department of Dramatic Writing (Class of 2022). Notable collaborations include the Kennedy Center American College Festival, New Harmony Project, Cornish College of the Arts, and Live Girls Theatre. She is a current board member of Rain City Projects and a current member of the Dramatist Guild.

Anuhea Brown

I'm Sorry About the Raw Eggs I Hid in Your Apartment (and/the/time/I/trimmed/ your/hair)

CHARACTERS:

RHEA   (Female/NB) Early thirties. High strung and
                   type A. Unapologetically strives to be in the
                   'right' in most scenarios. Extremely impulsive.

JOHN   (Male/NB) Early thirties. Speaks as he thinks.
                   Has a hard time finding words. Has a hard
                   time speaking his truth.

SETTING:

A warm summer night in a Western Desert.

NOTES:

/ Overlapping text

— Interruptions

Italicized / CAPITALIZED - Emphasis

The mountains loom in the distance. Moonlight. Hues of beige and orange rock. Their edges perforated from the experience of time.

The dirt reeks of something utterly hedonistic, something that has existed in the air for years. Almost so casually to the point that it is futile.

JOHN sits on a large red rock, he is rolling a marijuana cigarette.

For a moment he takes in his surroundings. For a moment he pretends to be John Wayne.

RHEA enters on stage wildly panting. She is clearly frustrated and out of breath.

JOHN: I thought people hiked in Seattle? I thought you hiked?

RHEA: (*panting*) Hiking isn't a personality trait—ok—get over it.

JOHN: How far away are we?

RHEA: It should be here right?

JOHN: Nah. I think it's farther up?

RHEA: You do?

JOHN: I mean that's what I remember?

RHEA: No I think you're wrong/

JOHN: You're gonna say I'm wrong.

RHEA: Well you're ALWAYS wrong.

JOHN: Now I'm always wrong?!

RHEA: I'm just saying this isn't the first time/

JOHN: I know this is isn't the first time we've gotten—

RHEA: YOU'VE gotten us lost./

JOHN: HERE WE GO—

RHEA: I just—I know what I'm talking about—see—look—

JOHN: It just has to be farther/

RHEA: Don't interrupt/

JOHN: I'm just saying I swear/

RHEA: Are you gonna listen to me? LOOK—BIG ROCK

RHEA crosses in between two mountains, that form a tiny path. She is extremely physical in proving her point.

RHEA: In between two mountains. South of the strip. You look and see the Luxor and then you should be here.

Silence. JOHN looks at the two mountains and the big rock.

He shrugs.

JOHN: I still think it's further up.

RHEA rolls her eyes. JOHN begins to stand on the rock.

He breathes in the polluted air of the desert sky. An array of twinkling lights.

JOHN feels like GOD among illuminated ants.

JOHN: Come up here with me.

RHEA: I'm ok.

JOHN: Come on. It feels good. Come on.

RHEA: I said I'm ok.

JOHN and RHEA actually look at each other for the first time.

JOHN: Do you have to pee? Because I have to PEE.

RHEA: I really do have to pee . . . BUT DON'T LOOK.

JOHN: (*smiling*) OK—that's—that's super unnecessary.

RHEA: What are you talking about?

JOHN: LIKE—I've seen your—you know what—before—a lot—many times—it's not new.

RHEA: WELLLLL that's exactly why—I think you should turn around because it isn't—NEW—so . . . so turn around.

JOHN is oddly perplexed, but listens and turns away from her.

JOHN: You're really not trying to see my thing?

RHEA: No I'm not trying to see your thing what??

JOHN: Well—I'm just pointing out ok—it would be a DOUBLE standard if you had hypothetically seen my THING You know . . . my ANACONDA My THUNDER FROM DOWN UNDER!

Silence.

JOHN: While I had peed . . .pissed . . . pissing.

RHEA: Keep talking, it's great.

JOHN: (*sighs*) Anyways—I'm gonna pee now.

JOHN begins to imitate RHEA.

JOHN: Doooooooon't LOOOOOOOK ok.

JOHN creeps into some god awful corner of the stage and turns around. He begins to unbuckle his pants.

JOHN: So—um—I—uh—I'm glad you agreed to grab drinks with me tonight.

RHEA: Coffee—

JOHN: Right—right—COFFEE—anyways—

RHEA: Please don't talk to me with your thing out.

JOHN: Right—Right—OK.

Silence. There's only the sound of pissing which oddly comforting.

RHEA: So you broke up with

JOHN: Yeah.

RHEA: Right.

JOHN: I mean it was good . . . until it wasn't.

RHEA: So did she do it or did you do it—or—WAIT—actually you won't tell me and you'll say it was MUTUAL.

JOHN: It was mutual.

RHEA: Right.

JOHN: I'm serious it was.

RHEA: Were you two serious?

JOHN: Like?

RHEA: Like we're getting old so . . .

JOHN: Like did I ask her to marry me?

RHEA: Did you?

JOHN: No?

Silence.

JOHN: Are you thinking about marriage?

RHEA: Ummmm . . . Not really, not anymore.

RHEA looks at JOHN. JOHN is faced away from RHEA.

JOHN: Not anymore?

Silence. JOHN thinks.

JOHN: What the hell does that even mean?

RHEA:It means when you have spent as much time as I have hoping for the inevitable, it becomes irrelevant. Like sun in the winter. Like pigs that fly. Like rain in the—

JOHN: Okay, okay, I get the analogy.

RHEA: Well if you got the analogy then I would be married. . . . Right John?

> *JOHN pauses. RHEA presses on.*

RHEA: RIGHT?

> *Beat.*

JOHN: I'm still pissing?

RHEA: Ok?

JOHN: So should I talk or?

RHEA: I don't know should you?

> *JOHN finishes and zips his pants. Just as JOHN is about to face RHEA; RHEA begins to turn away.*

RHEA: Actually, you know what? I'm gonna pee too now.

> *RHEA slides past JOHN. She begins to turn around and squat.*

JOHN: CLASSIC.

RHEA: What?

JOHN: A CLASSIC RHEA MOVE.

RHEA: What?

JOHN: Like a fucking game of cat and mouse—Tom and Jerry—bullshit. It's exhausting to repeat and HONESTLY we should skip this part—and just get to the part where we make out by the cave and pretend that this time will be different—and sure it will be good—it's always good—for some time—for some time it's GREAT. Like when I leave raw eggs around your apartment or when you end up sleeping on my floor because we talk so much . . . but I'll leave you—right?

RHEA: John.

JOHN: I'll leave you of course—I ALWAYS do—and you of course—you always resent that—you aren't too keen on the leaving part even though it happens a lot quite a bit—so much so that you think you'd be USED to it by now—but you never do—and then we get coffee—not DRINKS—no that would WILD—if we had just mutually decided that it would be best to numb the pain with LIQUOR rather than going through this again. SOBER.

RHEA: Would you cut it out—

JOHN: And we come here to where we went on our first date. When I had that jeep, the one with the almost busted tail light—and I told you—you WERE gonna be amazing at life—which is why I think—I think I always somewhat resent the fact that you RESENT me for leaving you. But we always end up coming here, and I always try to act SURPRISED And I pee and hide. And you pee. And then you get into how I'm the highlight of your life—

RHEA starts to cry. It's not super sudden but just happens, almost like she is sneezing tears.

JOHN: God. Now you're crying, I hate when you do that. It's ok. Come here. Right you're peeing, peeing and crying.

RHEA finishes peeing. She crosses and sits on the rock John was sitting on.

She can't really look at him. It's very apparent. She finds the marijuana cigarette on the rock and lights it.

JOHN: I'm just saying this because . . . well . . . because I wasn't lying about thinking you WERE gonna be amazing at life. And I still think that sometimes. Sometimes I *don't* if I'm being honest. But if we keep doing this—coffee—and hikes in the dark—then we'll do this wrong FOREVER. So if we do this, it has to be NEW. Completely new. Okay? You don't know me and I don't know you and we'll just find that again. I think. Right?

RHEA puffs.

JOHN: Can you please just say something?

RHEA: The cave is gone.

JOHN: What?

RHEA: It was plugged up three months ago. That's why we can't find it and that's why we don't see it.

JOHN: Wow . . . Wow. It's—it's gone and . . . You *knew*?

RHEA nods.

RHEA: So . . . Yeah. I just struggle with—I mean—you're right for once you're right.

RHEA: And maybe nature or the world agree's with you too.

JOHN: Because if it isn't here . . . if the cave doesn't exist.

RHEA: Than why should we?

JOHN: Ouch.

RHEA shrugs. JOHN rambles.

JOHN: Yeah. No. Yeah. That's—that's fair.

RHEA: And ALSO—you are not the highlight of my life. I don't think I've ever said that.

JOHN: Sureeeee ok.

RHEA: And if anything I'm the HIGHLIGHT OF YOUR LIFE.

JOHN: (*matter of factly*) You are.

RHEA: You're PROBABLY arguably my downfall.

JOHN: Marry me.

RHEA: What?

JOHN: I hate you. And I also love you. AND I wanna do this right—and I wanna marry you.

RHEA: Ok—but the cave—

JOHN: Fuck the cave. You tell me right now if you'd marry me. We don't have to disappear just because the world tells us we should.

Beat. JOHN looks at RHEA. RHEA looks at JOHN.

RHEA: Ok.

JOHN begins to smile. He may even laugh.

JOHN: I'll take 'Ok' for now . . . For now ok sounds good.

RHEA and JOHN join each other on the rock. They look at the view of the world . . . Then they look at each other. Within this look is a million words in a million times of how much they have said 'I love you' or "Come back to me" or "You are my home."

The look lingers and doesn't ever really seem to fade.

Lights fade.

BRIAN DANG (they/them) is a Vietnamese/Chinese playwright, teaching artist, and baby poet from Duwamish Territory (Seattle). Brian is a proud resident playwright at Parley. For Brian, writing is an act of envisioning an eventual communing, an opportunity to freeze time as we know it, and a reaching for joy.

Brian Dang

I'm afraid of sleep (or waking up), will you stay with me before I fall?

CHARACTER:

FETU   a (kind of) insomniac who talks through
                            the night to those who will listen.

SETTING:

Fetu's bedroom.

NOTES:

Originally performed by Fune Tautala and directed by Kiefer Harrington
for *RESILIENCE!: An AAPI 24-Hour Play Festival* on Zoom with Pork Filled
Productions. Thank you for the ephemeral, wonderful time together.

12:00 AM

> *FETU appears in front of the camera. They're live streaming.*

FETU: Is it working? Oh, yes, okay. We're live. Hi! Thanks for being here with me. If you've been here before you know the drill, I'm still really scared, but—

12:42 AM

> *FETU is in a different position, showing off their pajamas.*

FETU: —yeah they're my favorite pajamas, I wash them every other day to make sure I get to wear them. I have a silly feeling that they'll help. At least a little, y'know, to be comfortable. It doesn't hurt, it certainly wouldn't hurt, don't you think, I'd really like to not see it again, ever, ever—

1:37 AM

> *FETU has a guitar or ukulele (no need for it if not available).*

FETU: Hi. So this one goes out to John Mayer. I know Taylor just re-released *Red* so this is kind of bad timing, but . . . I'm feeling . . . romantic. There's this . . . girl . . . I might . . . like . . . no, no, that's silly, I shouldn't say that, anyway—here's the song.

> *FETU sings two verses to a John Mayer song. Somewhere, abruptly, it cuts—*

2:11 AM

> *FETU stands by a window (only if there is one in the bedroom).*

FETU: —been wondering how it gets in, when I'm asleep. Through my window? I don't even know what it *looks* like. But I do know what it sounds like. A whistle. The kind that gets dogs to stop. But something about it is off. Like the air is struggling to get through, like labored breathing or—

2:47 AM

> *FETU plays the sound of windchimes from their phone. It's not completely clear, and slightly disembodied. FETU is rocking, silently in a chair. Then, starts to move in unexpected ways. It appears as if they're lightly possessed or like there's an unseen puppeteer controlling them.*

There are a lot of small movements in the fingers, hands, and upper body, until the movement beings to crescendo and crescendo and— sometime, during the dance, an abrupt cut—

3:29 AM

FETU plays an audio book or podcast from their phone. It's a scary story. We listen to a brief portion together until they interrupt.

FETU: I listen to these stories. Exposure is a proven therapy. I don't think *my* demon looks like that though. It looks like something else. Something else—

4:03 AM

FETU is in a new position, laying in bed. We see FETU's eyes up close. They start to close slowly. And then they abruptly open again. The same way you catch yourself falling during a class or a boring movie. The moments that FETU's eyes are closed become longer and longer, and suddenly, a whistle sound fades in and out. The sudden wailing of the whistle sound becoming persistent and loud jostles FETU completely awake, horrified.

FETU: Oh, oh, god, why didn't you keep me awake? Why didn't you—

4:42 AM

A new position.

FETU: —you ever miss that time in childhood when you'd be taken to work by your parents if you had nowhere to go? I don't know how my mom did it, dealing with everything but still making sure I had a cheeseburger, at the very least. And she'd be doing her thing. Making people's hearts work again (literally). And I'd play pinball on the computer while I waited for hours . . . the purple yellow swirls, the boings, dings, and crashes are still in my head and at the end of it all, she'd bring me home, and I'd feel safe, and I wouldn't worry too much about tomorrow, and before I went to bed, she'd say don't let the thing come inside. She told me she's seen it before too. It was before I had my own. And then she'd say, I love you, and I'd say, I love you too, and then, and then—

4:46 AM

FETU reads from a book ("The Black Cat" by Edgar Allan Poe) but is barely awake. The words tumble and there are holes.

FETU: But may God shield and deliver me
!   the reverberation of   silence,
     I was   a cry,
                                        a child,
          one long, loud, and continuous scream,
               a howl—   half of
                                        hell,   from
throats   of   demons

.

     my own thoughts   stagger
                         the party

               toiling
                    with gore,   before the eyes

                                        me   and
     whose   voice had
     the monster   !

4:59 AM

A maximum of 7–10 seconds. FETU sits in a chair, eyes completely closed. The whistle sound throughout, persistent and loud. Something dark approaches. Abruptly, cut—

5:10 AM

A new position.

FETU: I wish I had Taco Bell. I should get Taco Bell.

FETU looks through the GrubHub on his phone.

FETU: "Nacho Cheese Doritos® Locos Tacos" for $2.86 . . .? Oh shit . . .

5:29 AM

FETU: It's so late. Or early. Is there a word for what this time is? Not literally, but what it feels like? I wish I could flip through time like a slide projector just—a click and clunk—and be back as a child at the apex of the arc on a swing-set, higher than I'll ever be, a 2 second moment, or push forward into tomorrow. Click. Clunk. I'm worried when I wake, the thing will be there. Watching me unable to move like a sack of old rice: unsure whether to throw it away. But I have a mantra. I have a mantra. 5, 4, 3, 2, 1. Get up. 5, 4, 3, 2, 1. Get up. It might work this time.

7:00 AM

FETU is very close to the camera.

FETU: I think this is what they call dawn. I think I might try to lay my head down. Because you're still here. And I trust you to stay with me, at least, for a little while. Watch out for me.

FETU gets into bed and pulls the covers over. Sleeps.

end of play.

BRET FETZER's plays range from sardonic romcoms to magic realist fables to compressed revisionist Greek tragedies to experimental collages about the history of torture, Medieval animal trials, and Camille Paglia. His feature film *My Last Year with the Nuns* (adapted from the solo show by Matt Smith, which Bret also directed) is available through Prime Video. He also writes original fairy tales.

Bret Fetzer

Capsule

CHARACTERS:

NARRATOR	a metaphysical/metatheatrical device
ALEKSEI LEONOV	a cosmonaut in trouble
PAVEL BELYAEV	a frantic scientist on the ground
DAGMAR KRAUS	a confused professional proofreader

SETTING:

ALEKSEI sits in a wooden chair in the center of the room. There are no other setpieces. He is dressed in normal street clothes; no attempt should be made to realistically depict the circumstances of this play. ALEKSEI stares forward, paralyzed with anxiety and loss.

NOTES:

PAVEL and DAGMAR should only be voices, ideally speaking through a microphone. ALEKSEI should be the visual focus of the play.

None of the characters of this play speak with an accent, unless they are pronouncing words foreign to them.

The NARRATOR, much like the Stage Manager of Thornton Wilder's *Our Town*, both comments on and interacts with the world of the other characters. However, it may be helpful to think of him/her as a preternatural being, a guardian angel perhaps; or as the manifestation of a part of ALEKSEI's mind.

The NARRATOR enters and addresses the audience.

NARRATOR: This is Aleksei Arkhipovich Leonov. He is not sitting in a wooden chair. His seat is made of aluminum, copper, plastic, and steel. It rests—not on the floor of this theater—but inside of a capsule, that was released from the nose of a rocket, launched from the Baikonur Cosmodrome on March 18, 1965. His capsule is now floating in orbit around the earth. He's wearing a suit made of plastic, metal mesh, and thick layers of polyester. It's white, with the insignia of the Soviet space program and the USSR itself on the breastplate. When—two hours and thirty-four minutes before this moment—he buckled himself in, he closed a curved piece of clear but amazingly strong polymer resin over his face, forming an airtight seal with the rest of his helmet. For the next 23 hours, he will breathe nothing but recirculated air, which will gradually come to have a slightly chemical taste. It's a strange thing to be able to taste the air. It isn't natural. It isn't good.

PAVEL: Aleksei?

NARRATOR: For the moment, the air is tasteless, though the sound of it rushing in and out of his lungs, which Aleksei can hear resonating in his helmet, reminds him that he is dependent on seven tanks, which contain approximately 30 hours worth of oxygen. There were originally going to be 34 hours worth, but those four hours of air made the capsule too heavy. They had to be cut.

PAVEL: We're doing what we can. We're insisting. She'll be here any moment.

NARRATOR: This is the fifth time the Soviet Union has sent a human being into space.

PAVEL: The authorities are not heartless. They will let her come in.

NARRATOR: This is the first time that Aleksei Arkhipovich Leonev has ever been alone.

PAVEL: Aleksei? (*Pause.*) Aleksei?

ALEKSEI: (*barely audible*) Name.

PAVEL: What? (*to someone else in the room*) I think—ah—Aleksei? Did you say something? (*Pause.*) I think he—Aleksei, I am Pavel Belyaev. We shook hands this morning. Is that what you asked? Pavel. My name is Pavel. Aleksei?

NARRATOR: Aleksei Leonov has two brothers and seven sisters.

PAVEL: (*to someone else in the room*) Maybe he was just moaning.

NARRATOR: He shared a small apartment with six friends, in a city with a population of seven million people.

PAVEL: (*to someone else in the room*) Where are they?

NARRATOR: He spent five years in the constant company of twenty other space program recruits.

PAVEL: Aleksei, they have her downstairs. She's coming up.

NARRATOR: In the isolation tests, he was never more than ten feet away from another human being.

PAVEL: She's coming up.

NARRATOR: Unable to see them, unable to hear them, to touch them, to smell or taste them, he could—unconsciously, but absolutely—sense that other people were there, even through concrete walls.

PAVEL: Any moment now . . .

NARRATOR: But now, for the first time in his life, Aleksei is alone.

PAVEL: (*to DAGMAR*) Sit here. Speak to him.

DAGMAR: I don't—what is going on—

> *At the sound of DAGMAR's voice, ALEKSEI begins using sign language, signing, "Don't leave me alone."*

PAVEL: Into here.

DAGMAR: Where am I?

PAVEL: Aleksei? She's here. (*to DAGMAR*) Speak to him.

DAGMAR: Aleksei?

NARRATOR: Her name is Dagmar Kraus, and she doesn't speak any Russian. She works for a German publishing firm. She's speaking German, and none of the technicians understand her.

DAGMAR: Aleksei? Hello?

NARRATOR: The only available translator doesn't have enough security clearance to enter the control room. Of course, neither does Dagmar.

DAGMAR: Aleksei?

NARRATOR: No one knows who makes these decisions.

PAVEL: (*to DAGMAR*) He stopped speaking twenty minutes ago.

NARRATOR: She has no idea what this technician is saying.

DAGMAR: Aleksei, this is Dagmar.

NARRATOR: Aleksei has a German vocabulary of 25 words, ranging from "please" to "pantyhose," and he has forgotten all of them.

DAGMAR: Aleksei, are you there?

NARRATOR: Bitte.

DAGMAR: Why aren't you speaking to me?

NARRATOR: Strumpfwaren.

DAGMAR: (*to PAVEL*) Is it broken?

PAVEL: Don't stop.

NARRATOR: Aleksei and Dagmar speak mostly through sign language.

DAGMAR: Aleksei, they're scaring me. Are you there? Are you still alive?

NARRATOR: Because both of their mothers were deaf.

DAGMAR: Aleksei, please speak.

NARRATOR: His mother is now dead.

DAGMAR: Aleksei.

NARRATOR: Hers lives in East Berlin

DAGMAR: Aleksei, I love you.

NARRATOR: (*to ALEKSEI*) Ich. Liebe. Dich.

> *ALEKSEI signs "I love you."*

DAGMAR: Where are you?

NARRATOR: (*to ALEKSEI*) She's calling to you.

DAGMAR: I love you.

NARRATOR: (*to ALEKSEI*) Ich. Liebe. Dich.

> *ALEKSEI again signs "I love you."*

> *During the following, the NARRATOR may very slowly tip ALEKSEI's chair back, to the side, forward, and so on.*

DAGMAR: Aleksei, if you can hear me, tap. Like this.

> *She taps twice on the microphone.*

PAVEL: Don't do that!

DAGMAR: Aleksei?

> *She taps again.*

PAVEL: No! Nein! Nein!

> *In the control room, he grabs her hands.*

DAGMAR: Let go of me!

> *The NARRATOR taps twice.*

> *Pause.*

PAVEL: That's brilliant.

DAGMAR: Aleksei?

The NARRATOR taps twice.

PAVEL: Aleksei, can you hear me?

The NARRATOR taps twice.

PAVEL: (*to someone else in the room*) Fantastic! Get her out of here.

DAGMAR: What—

PAVEL: Aleksei, let's establish a code. Tap once for no, twice for yes. Do
   you understand? (*Pause.*) Aleksei? (*Pause.*) Shit—bring her back in here.
   Shit. Aleksei, I apologize. I am very stupid.

DAGMAR: What are you doing? Why are you—

PAVEL: Bitte, fraulein. Bitte.

DAGMAR: What is going on?

PAVEL: I don't know any more German. Talk to him. In here.

He taps on the microphone.

DAGMAR: Aleksei? Hello?

The NARRATOR taps twice.

PAVEL: Aleksei, I apologize, I will not send her away again. She is listening
   to you. And though I don't know what she's saying, I can tell that she
   loves you very much. Very, very much. And she wants you to finish your
   mission and come home. Dagmar?

DAGMAR: Aleksei, I don't know what he wants me to say.

PAVEL: Aleksei, can you hear me?

The NARRATOR taps twice.

DAGMAR taps twice on the microphone.

PAVEL: That was Dagmar tapping back to you. Do you understand what I
   said before? Twice for yes, once for no?

The NARRATOR taps twice.

PAVEL: Are you tapping twice because every other time you've tapped twice?

The NARRATOR taps once.

PAVEL: Oh thank god. I do not believe in God, but Aleksei, I believe in you.

DAGMAR: Aleksei, I love you.

NARRATOR: (*to ALEKSEI*) Ich. Liebe. Dich.

PAVEL: Aleksei, if Dagmar is here with you, are you able to leave the capsule?

The NARRATOR taps twice.

DAGMAR taps twice back.

PAVEL: That was Dagmar again. She loves you very much. Aleksei, have you inflated the airlock?

The NARRATOR taps twice.

DAGMAR taps twice back.

PAVEL: All the tapping is Dagmar. She is still here. (*to DAGMAR*) Speak.

DAGMAR: I love you.

NARRATOR: (*to ALEKSEI*) Ich. Liebe. Dich.

PAVEL: (*to DAGMAR*) Say that as much as you want. Aleksei? Can you unbuckle your belt?

The NARRATOR taps twice.

DAGMAR: Aleksei, this morning—

PAVEL: Just—(*In the control room, he touches DAGMAR and gestures to her to be quiet.*)—one moment. Aleksei, please unbuckle your belt, and let me know when you have risen from your seat.

When ALEKSEI has stood—and his movement should be very slow— the NARRATOR taps twice.

PAVEL: Wonderful. Aleksei, are you ready to go into the airlock?

The NARRATOR taps twice.

PAVEL: Wait, hold— (*to someone else in the room*) I think, when he goes in the airlock, I don't think he can tap any more—Aleksei, can you make a clucking, a clicking noise with your tongue? Like this?

He clicks with his tongue, twice.

DAGMAR: What—

She tries, but can't make the noise.

PAVEL: Dagmar wants to click at you, but she can't. Aleksei?

The NARRATOR clicks back, twice.

PAVEL exhales with relief.

PAVEL: You will have to teach Dagmar how to do that when you get back. Aleksei, I want you to open the hatch, and step into the airlock. When you have closed the hatch behind you, click twice.

When ALEKSEI has taken two steps, the NARRATOR clicks twice.

DAGMAR again tries to click, but can't.

PAVEL: Aleksei, is your safety line secure?

The NARRATOR clicks twice.

PAVEL: Aleksei, are you ready to unseal the exit to the airlock?

The NARRATOR clicks twice.

PAVEL: Aleksei, I want you to unseal the exit. When you have lifted yourself out of the airlock, click twice.

ALEKSEI takes four steps.

The NARRATOR clicks twice.

PAVEL: Aleksei, you are a great, great man. I worship you. I love you almost as much as Dagmar does. (*to DAGMAR*) You don't understand me, but Aleksei is floating in space, outside of the capsule. He will drift in space for five minutes, held by a line of woven nylon fibers, and then climb back in. Please, speak to him. Bitte.

DAGMAR: Aleksei? Are you there?

ALEKSEI stares out into the audience.

The NARRATOR clicks twice.

DAGMAR: Aleksei, this morning, when you dressed to leave the apartment, I was awake. I pretended to be asleep, because I was afraid to say goodbye to you. I thought if I said goodbye, I would never see you again. I listened to how you put on your shirt. I listened to how you pulled on your pants. I listened to you shave. I was afraid I would never hear the sound of you shaving again. When you left, I could still smell you on the sheets, and I took all the sheets off the bed and I put them in a box so I could keep that smell forever and ever because I was afraid I would never smell you again. Please come back to me, Aleksei. Please let me smell your body again.

NARRATOR: For the first time, as he drifts in the airless vaccuum, Aleksei Leonov looks down, upon the clouds and the oceans and the green and brown continents, all the countries of the world, all the human beings that walk and crawl and dance and make love upon the face of the Earth, and he no longer feels alone.

ALEKSEI: Ich . . . liebe . . . dich.

Blackout.

MIKKI GILLETTE is a trans woman playwright. She was named one of Portland, OR's 25 Most Influential Artists by Willamette Week magazine. Her play *American Girl* was featured in American Theatre and was produced by Fuse Theatre in April '23. Her show *The Queers* enjoyed a sold-out run in March '22, and her show *My Perfectly Valid Objections* finished a sold-out, extended run with Salt and Sage in February '23. Mikki's play *Blonde on a Bum Trip* will premiere in Portland in May 2024. She was a member of the Ashland New Plays Festival 2022 New Voices Cohort, and Profile Theatre's LGBTQIA+ Community Profile Cohort. Learn more at: mikkigillette.com.

Mikki Gillette

There's a Word for That

CHARACTERS:

POE
a trans woman in her 20s, quirky and light-hearted by nature, the difficulties of living and dating as a trans woman have heightened her suspicion and vigilance.

EDDIE
a cis man in his 20s, though kind and empathetic, he can be sensitive to critiques that counter his self-image.

SETTING:

A restaurant in a U.S. city. Present day.

NOTES:

A stroke (/) marks the point of interruption in overlapping dialogue.

A dash (—) marks the halting of a thought.

Poe and Eddie sit in a restaurant.

POE: Sometimes people ask me, like, "What's your favorite band? Or movie?" and I don't know how to answer, you know?

EDDIE: You don't?

POE: (*embarrassed*) No, because—never mind. It's not really / important

EDDIE: Huh? . . . You can / say if you want

POE: What I meant is, before I—(*uncomfortable*) Transitioned . . . I would watch, like, the worst deep cut "Transformers" film over and over, probably as some gender chemotherapy exercise, and then blather on about the / cinematography

EDDIE: (*surprised*) Oh right . . . you're / trans

POE: Um . . . yeah. I mean, I totally / messaged you that

EDDIE: Sure . . . I / remember now

POE: You have a weird expression / all the sudden

EDDIE: What? . . . I think this is just / my face

POE: I disclosed within like, five minutes of you / messaging

EDDIE: I know. Sorry, I just forgot . . . Please don't worry about—I mean, I'm enjoying getting to know / you

POE: (*uneasy*) Okay . . . I guess my point was, it's hard to tell how much of my taste was authentic, and what was just, like, conforming to / expectations

EDDIE: Right . . . well, do you still like Transformers / movies

POE: No . . . they're like "Triumph of the Will," but with Mark Wahlberg, you know? So even worse . . . wait—you don't like those movies, / do you

EDDIE: No, I also prefer "Triumph of the Will."

Pause.

POE: Um . . . that was a joke, right?

EDDIE: Yes.

POE: Oh good . . . always have to be gauging the "potential threat level," right? (*quickly, nervous*) Haha.

EDDIE: (*laughs, uneasy*) Um, did you say "threat / level"?

POE: Sorry, you can just pretend that / didn't happen

EDDIE: Did you mean—you weren't saying / that I'm

POE: No . . . I mean, not more than other, you know, cis, / straight

EDDIE: I didn't do something wrong, did I? We're just talking about, um, Mark / Wahlberg, and

POE: I know. Please, don't mind me—

EDDIE: Okay /

POE: Although, the "just talking" period "is" where one gauges threats, right? Before it's too late?

EDDIE: Technically, I guess—wait, what are we / discussing

POE: Nothing. Ugh, I shouldn't have brought up my transition. Now all / I can think about

EDDIE: (*compassionate*) Oh, I don't want you to feel uncomfortable . . . I mean, we're having a good time, / right

POE: Yes, totally . . . Although earlier you were, like—(*imitating Eddie*) "Oh, right. You're / trans"

EDDIE: Um, I don't actually talk like / that

POE: And I thought, oh great. He's going to go home and post a GIF of the stupid Family Guy dog throwing up under a "Tonight's date" caption, or / something

EDDIE: (*uncomfortable*) I wouldn't do—um, why would / you think

POE: Or, fuck, maybe he's going to post my profile photo on some gross subreddit, saying—(*imitating, only coarser*) "Watch out for this dude, / guys"

EDDIE: I've never done—I don't really sound like that when I / talk, do I?

POE: Hmm? No—or, I mean, kind of? Let's talk about something / else

EDDIE: Okay . . . on your profile, you said you like rock climbing, right?

POE: Oh, um . . . that was a lie.

EDDIE: Huh?

POE: I, you know, made that up.

EDDIE: Oh . . . why would / you

POE: (*sighs, impatient*) In dating profiles, I noticed everyone claims to like athletic, outdoor activities. I assumed they were all lying, so I just decided to lie, / also

EDDIE: You really thought one hundred percent of the people on / those apps were

POE: Basically. (*groans, head in hands*) Look, I wasn't saying you personally would post horrible, transphobic shit about me, but the things I described before have happened to girls I know. Also, I saw that you got uncomfortable when I brought up the Family Guy / thing, so

EDDIE: (*evasive*) I was probably just surprised at being, um, accused, or /
. . .

POE: I wasn't accusing you. I was . . . (*self-conscious*) Um, doom spiraling, which is always a successful first date strategy.

EDDIE: (*compassionate*) I didn't really notice the—we're having a good time, right? Remember the "Triumph of the Will" jokes?

Poe forces a weak laugh before collapsing on the table.

EDDIE: Um . . . Poe?

POE: (*muffled*) I'm okay.

EDDIE: (*hiding concern*) Oh good . . . And did you maybe want to, um, sit /
up

Poe groans, then slowly pushes herself up again.

POE: I'm sure this looks kind of suboptimal, but when you consider how hard it is to date as a trans woman, I think my performance here is / not bad

EDDIE: (*hiding confusion*) Um, / sure

POE: It's like, "Well, every movie I watched growing up suggested I'll either murder other people, or be murdered myself, because I like wearing dresses, but I'm sure this evening will be / fun"

EDDIE: Are you sure you're feeling / okay

POE: "I hope I don't get doxxed tonight because the person I'm seeing feels upset about my gender identity. Also, did I remember / my keys?"

EDDIE: That sounds really hard.

POE: I don't know. Other girls do it all the time. I should probably just be a nun, or something.

EDDIE: (*slightly guilty*) No, I mean it. What you're saying is true, / and

POE: "Trans nun—queering the church from the inside." That would actually be pretty awesome . . . except I'd have to live in a convent, I guess, and go to church a lot.

EDDIE: I appreciate you sharing . . . everything.

POE: Right, what better getting to know you chat could there be?

EDDIE: No, I mean it . . . Just to clarify, though: you don't think I would ever be the kind of—I mean, I'm not like those / guys who

POE: What?

EDDIE: I'm saying, it's not like we just met at a party. We messaged for a while, and I'm not all, "I love to doxx / people"

POE: I guess. But I don't think anyone's like, "I love to doxx people." If they were, we could stop them before / they

EDDIE: That's true . . . it sounds like it's hard for you to trust people, though, and I wouldn't want you to feel—I mean, I'm not saying "I'm perfect," or whatever, but I hope you're feeling okay here with me.

POE: Yeah, this is—it's actually kind of nice.

EDDIE: Oh good . . . for a minute there, I was afraid that when you were sharing your worst-case scenarios, they were, like, some coded reference to how you saw me.

POE: (*hiding annoyance*) Oh, right.

EDDIE: "Threat level" and all, you / know

POE: What about "threat level"?

EDDIE: Well, it implied that I'm . . . somehow / a threat

POE: You are. Women like me get harassed, assaulted and killed by the men we date.

EDDIE: I know, but—and I'm not sure how this conversation led us here— not every man, and not I, specifically, would do that.

    Pause.

POE: Wow . . . if the worst thing that could happen to me on a date was someone accurately noting that I could ruin their life without suffering any consequences myself—(*daydreaming*) I can imagine paying a sex worker just to role play that / scenario

EDDIE: Okay . . . I guess what I meant was—(*vulnerable*) We're on a date. I was hoping you'd be . . . interested, at least a little, in me as a person.

POE: (*embarrassed*) Oh, sorry . . . I got a little fixated on, I guess, being victimized, or—but, no, you're right. Let's live in the moment.

EDDIE: (*uncertain*) So does that mean—?

POE: Yeah, um . . . what are your hobbies?

EDDIE: Hobbies? I play softball. I'm in a fantasy football league. I / like

POE: Very sports oriented.

EDDIE: I guess . . . oh, right. You think athletics don't exist.

POE: I remain skeptical.

EDDIE: And what about you? When you're not enduring dates with cis men, what / do you like

POE: (*playful*) You know the word "cis" . . . I'm impressed.

EDDIE: It's 2023.

POE: Tell that to Dave Chapelle.

> *Eddie laughs, then pauses, guiltily.*

EDDIE: (*embarrassed, with difficulty*) When you said that thing earlier, about the dog from the Family / Guy

POE: (*nervous, suspicious*) Yes?

EDDIE: The reason I looked uncomfortable was . . . I had a friend, and we sometimes shared—it was dumb, like an inside / joke

POE: What are you saying? Did you share it when—was it / about trans women

EDDIE: Not always, but . . . famous ones, / or

> *Poe stands, upset.*

POE: This has been delightful. I'm so glad you wanted / to meet

> *Eddie stands, nervous.*

EDDIE: Please wait, Poe.

POE: (*gathering her things*) Don't let me keep you from your "inside / jokes"

EDDIE: The reason I said that just now is because—you may not even care, but . . . you've helped me think a lot about, you know, the ways I've been shitty around this stuff / and

POE: Transphobia.

EDDIE: Right. / That's—

POE: Transmisogyny.

EDDIE: Um . . . / okay

POE: It's the word that describes when people are assholes to trans women—(*quietly*) Like the dog on The Family Guy.

EDDIE: Right, that's what I'm talking—you don't have to stay, but . . . I just wanted to tell you I listened, and I'm sorry I did that before.

Poe, surprised, pauses. Her anger cooling, she warily sits again. Eddie sits, as well.

POE: I accept your apology, I guess.

EDDIE: Thank you.

POE: That sounded weird, like I was accepting it on behalf of all—anyway, I appreciate your honesty.

EDDIE: I'm glad. (*pause*) You didn't share what your hobbies were before.

POE: I go on dating apps to find men to doxx.

EDDIE: Um . . . that was a—you're joking, / right

POE: Yes, I am. I sing in a trans choir.

EDDIE: Really? That sounds nice.

POE: (*droll*) Wait till you've heard us before you say that.

EDDIE: (*flirty*) I wouldn't mind having the chance.

Poe smiles, a little surprised. The two pick up their menus, intrigued.

KI GOTTBERG, Seattle native, has been writing, directing, acting, and teaching for decades. A graduate of UofW Professional Actor Training Program, member of Actors Equity/SAG/AFTRA, Ki has performed (Seattle Rep, Intiman, ACT, Upstart Crow, etc.), and directed around the Northwest. Her voice-over work spans diverse genre including books, commercials, narrations, etc. Her plays have been produced in New York, LA, San Francisco; in Seattle at Empty Space, New City, Intiman, The Womb, Seattle Rep, festivals, etc. She was Artistic Director of the Merc Playhouse in Twisp, WA for 4.5 years; made it rock.

A recipient of awards, commissions, grants including the national $25,000 NEA/TCG Individual Artist Fellowship and a local Artist Trust Fellowship for playwriting, Ki was professor and the first Chair of Performing Arts/ Arts Leadership at Seattle University, retiring Emerita in 2022. During those 35 years, beginning as a part-time adjunct with no theater space, Ki exults to have been instrumental in building the Theatre program and the Lee Center for the Arts at SU.

Ki currently performs her one-woman show *Frontier* about her mixed-race heritage for salon audiences, and is writing/acting with her Madcap Melodrama 'live radio' troupe in Port Townsend.

Theatre should discomfit, titillate, posit big ideas. We squirm with possibilities!

Ki Gottberg

Safe

CHARACTERS:

O   easy-going longtime pal of Bit, a freelancer.

BIT   works from home, somewhat fastidious.

BIRD   a bird, does bird stuff like scratch, peck, stand
                          as if frozen, squawk, rise up on toes and flap,
                          gobble, croak, coo, etc. No "bird costume"
                          other than suggestive.

SETTING:

The apartment of Bit: there is a 'window' and a couch.

NOTES:

The more "UberBird" the bird is, the better. Precise bird movement and
behavior.

O and Bit are sitting at home on the sofa. Throughout, O has a more casual acceptance of the situation, whereas Bit becomes more agitated.

O: Hey. Ya wanna go to the store with me?

BIT: No way. I get my stuff delivered now.

O: You let someone pick your produce?

BIT: Damn right. You aware? Disease? You seen those hoods hangin' around down at Shit Mart, lookin' like they'd just as soon slice and dice your stuff as smoke another spliff? I stay right here with my door locked and wait for the big green truck to bring me my stuff.

O: They don't know how to pick a good avocado.

BIT: You seen all the folks feeling everything in the produce aisle in between stickin' their fingers down the back of their pants after they stuff em up their noses? I want the rubber glove service of grocery delivery!

O: You are getting nuts.

BIT: Yeah, in a can with a seal.

A flapping sound and a big bird person 'flies' through the 'window' and lands on the carpet. No bird costume, just bird actions.

O: Jesus! That things' huge!

BIT: (*freaked*) Get out! Get out!

Bit attempts to shoo the Bird out. The Bird pecks at Bit, O, and pushes them back on the sofa. Both Bit and O pull their legs up and huddle on the sofa like on an island. The bird pecks and scratches around, ignoring them, making little cooing and clucking noises as it cruises around the sofa.

O: Whoa. You can't screw around with that one. A serious bird. What kind do you think she is?

BIT: "She"? How do you know it's a "she"? And now you are into ornithology? What Kind is It? FREAKISHLY LARGE! And how about helping me get 'her' out of here? Birds are disgustingly dirty things. I don't want that in here.

O: I don't see what you can do about it. It's gi-normous.

BIT: If we both run at it, it'll fly back out to where it came from.

O: . . . I don't know . . . oooh . . . look what it just did on the carpet.

BIT: (*looking at it—grossed out*) I'm gonna be sick . . .

O: Jesus, it's just some bird crap, Bit. I mean, it's large. . . . We can let it dry and vacuum it right up.

BIT: (*still staring at it*) That pile is so big it would choke my sucker thing.

O: If you say so.

BIT: (*pulls herself out of her state*) We got to get it out! OUT! And what's with you, anyway, acting like it's all normal to have an outsized bird suddenly appear in the room and attack me?

O: Attack you?! Uh, I think it's an equal op deal here with both of us. And you leaving a window open that wide? All the warnings say "a crack".

BIT: Warnings? I haven't seen any more warnings . . .

O: The City Safety Commission has papered every bus stop with flyers! They've got safety banners over all the freeways now! (*O acts these warnings out in a manic fashion*) "Gloves n glasses!"; "Carry newspaper for seating"; "Overhangs Protect!"; "Look, Think, then Move"; "No Bright Colors, especially Reds"; "Report All Contacts"; "Shoe Purification Pool Use Required"; and on and on and . . .

BIT: (*interrupting, moaning*) And WHEN will it end?! And WHERE? I REFUSE TO BE ADAPTABLE.

O: Hey, when was the last time you went outside? That's the problem with you work-from-home geeks. Have you even looked out the window?

BIT: (*suddenly alert*) What do you mean?

O: Things have been changing out there.

BIT: What do you mean, "changing"?

O: Changing. I've seen some really large 'small animals' recently . . .

> *The Bird suddenly becomes agitated and makes more sound, marching around the sofa and waggling its head. It pecks at and nudges them, pushing them together. Bit attempts to beat it back, and the bird becomes quite aggressive, finally calms down and goes back to its scratching and clucking routine.*

BIT: Jesus! What is going on? We need help. This bird is a monster! Do you have your phone?

O: Didn't you hear about the cell towers? Some giant Osprey built a nest so huge that it literally collapsed a tower: took out two others when it fell. The whole things' a mess.

BIT: What!?

O: Supposedly they'll get it worked out in another week. Their first priority right now is dealing with the enormo ants that tunneled under the freeway and took out that bridge . . . Gods, Bit, you are totally out of touch, and now this bird.

BIT: (*shocked*) "And now this bird?" "And now this bird?!!"

O: Calm down. It's all been on TV, or don't you watch?

BIT: Of course I don't watch! Porno Vampire fuck scenes spliced in between endless end-of-the-world weather and volcano eruption stories? 'Reality' shows about people forcing other people to do push-ups and wear cute clothes?! Competing Chefs?! I know we are doomed, why would I want to WATCH ?!!

> *The Bird pecks Bit and squawks.*

BIT: Ouch! Stop that!

> *Bit hits wildly at the bird. The Bird rises up, flaps madly, crowing, bobbing and gobbling.*

O: (*attempting to calm Bit*) Bit, It's just a bird!

> *Bit can't believe O's attitude. The bird continues to squawk, and now jumps onto the sofa between them and spreads its "wings". They try to get away, but the bird subdues them with aggressive pecking and wing work.*

O and BIT: ow! OW!

O: This bird means business!

BIT: This can't be happening!

O: It is!

> *Now with insistent cooing, the bird 'nests' and settles on the sofa with the two friends under the bird wings as if chicks. A pause. They stage whisper.*

O: OMG, do you think she thinks we are her babies?

BIT: I don't know what the fuck 'she' "thinks". I think we are in danger!

O: It's just a bird . . .

BIT: A giant chicken/pigeon/turkey thing that is controlling humans is not "just a bird", O!

O: It's kind of nice under here . . . fluffy . . . toasty and all.

BIT: Are you on dope?

O: (*snuggling*) Feels kinda good . . .

BIT: (*beginning to succumb to the warmth*) We . . . we have to get out of here. . . . I mean, yeah, the fluff . . . ooh the fluff . . . ooh . . . but what's gonna happen next? Her giant rat pal comes to visit?! She makes us eat bugs?

O: (*dreamy*) Ooh. I hate rats.

They are both really zoning into the bird nest warmth.

BIRD: (*in a strange accent? Sing-song? With added clucks and coos*) Chickies . . . my chicks. . . . I am your mama now. Your warm feather mama.
Hear my deep bird peep. (*pause—all listen*)
Go to sleep. Go to sleep.
Good little chickies go to sleep.
Dream your dreams, my squab-lings. (*joyous squawk of motherhood*)
Scratching and pecking. Yes, yes.
Tomorrow I will ralph pigeon milk into your desperate little beaks.
Tomorrow we find a fat termite—crunch crunch . . . Oh my chicks! My own little chickies! Tomorrow you will fly.

O: (*dreamy*) A big fat termite . . . (*giggles*) I hope she doesn't have any rat friends. I hate rats . . . big rats . . .

BIT: (*succumbing*) Oh god, oh god . . .

O: (*snuggling deeper*) mmmmm . . . termites. Big . . . fat . . . termites.

BIT: At least . . . (*a tiny flurry of worry*) O, are you still awake? O?
(*soft bird sounds, Bit surrenders*)
At least . . . at least we are safe . . .
(*slow fade w bird cooing, clucking, etc.*)

    The End

__EMILY HAVER__ (she/her) is a playwright, director, producer, and actor who also dabbles in film. She has a B.A. in Theatre from Seattle University and an M.A. in Intercultural Communication Studies from Shanghai Theatre Academy. Recently produced short plays include *The Happiest Day* (Taipei Shorts 5) and *We're All Trash* (Taipei Fringe Festival and Taipei Shorts 4). Originally from Seattle, Emily spent some of her teen years near Guangzhou, lived in Shanghai for two years, and is currently based out of Taipei. In Taipei, she writes for an educational magazine by day and supports the development of new plays as a producer for Taipei Shorts (and eats too many mangoes) by night. As an artist Emily collaborates across cultures, making ensemble and experimentation-based work that provokes social questions and is emotionally grounded. Her work is all about people—she uses truthfulness and intimacy to connect audiences to stories that feel both specific and universal. Emily is deeply passionate about authentically and lovingly telling stories about women and queer communities and hopes that her work makes people feel more alive and a little less alone in the world.

Emily Haver

little moons

CHARACTERS:

YOUNG WOMAN   nervously hopeful.

YOUNG MAN   ready (but scared).

SETTING:

Outdoors during a solar eclipse.

NOTES:

This play is about love and magic and the moon, but it is not sentimental. These characters have wants and the stakes are high. It's magical, but it's <u>real</u>. While written for a "young man" and "young woman," this is not important in the staging. People of all genders and in any combination can play these parts, because anyone can fall in love. They can be any age, but should have a youngness of spirit.

Outdoors, a warm late summer morning—two luxurious armchairs are set center stage. It is that special morning brightness when anything is possible. Slowly and continuously through the play it gets darker and darker, with tiny half-moon shadows eventually appearing onstage. A record player is playing Debussy's "Clair de lune" for the entirety of the play. Two figures are in the armchairs—a man and a woman. Both are wearing Japanese skincare face masks—hydrated skin is important when everything is about to change.

YOUNG MAN: This is it.

YOUNG WOMAN: We're here.

YOUNG MAN: So now we wait?

YOUNG WOMAN: Now we wait.

Beat. It's all very new.

YOUNG WOMAN: I wasn't sure you would come.

YOUNG MAN: I wasn't entirely certain you'd be here either.

YOUNG WOMAN: (*searching*) But I hoped you would.

Beat. It's a little awkward.

YOUNG MAN: How long are we supposed to keep these on for? You're the expert after all.

YOUNG WOMAN: 20 minutes, I think? It should time out perfectly with— well, this is actually my first time. So I'm not entirely sure.

YOUNG MAN: Oh, you've never done this before? You seemed so confident. This is my first time too. It's exciting.

YOUNG WOMAN: It *is* exciting, isn't it? The newness. It feels like my heart is exploding, or that I'm about to vomit. In a good way. But one thing I've always wondered . . . why are people so obsessed with firsts? Booze, kisses, loves. I think things tend to improve vastly after the first.

YOUNG MAN: To me, it's because you're inviting something new into the universe. Firsts are an act of creation, love, invitation—

YOUNG WOMAN: —proclaiming to the world: I CAN CHANGE.

YOUNG MAN: Precisely.

YOUNG WOMAN: But that's also why seconds, and thirds, and fourths, and 100ths are important too. Because they are the ones that say—I can grow. I can care. I'm staying. Watch me.

YOUNG MAN: A challenge.

YOUNG WOMAN: Yes.

YOUNG MAN: Which is *why* the first act also matters—because without it there is no 100th. Someone has to be brave. Someone has to start the caring.

YOUNG WOMAN: I think this is brave. Us. What we're doing.

YOUNG MAN: It's kinda scary.

YOUNG WOMAN: That's what makes us brave. (*Beat.*) Or stupid.

YOUNG MAN: Stupid-brave.

YOUNG WOMAN: (*laughing*) Brave-stupid.

YOUNG MAN: Do you think anyone else has done this before, in the history of the universe?

YOUNG WOMAN: I have no idea.

YOUNG MAN: I think that finally we're the right people, in the right time and right place. Doing exactly what we're supposed to be doing. (*reaching out and holding her hand*) Maybe all of time has led up to this very moment.

YOUNG WOMAN: Lots of people have held hands before. (*Beat.*) Lots of people have felt this before.

YOUNG MAN: But like this? We're new.

YOUNG WOMAN: I like that idea. That this is new. That there's been a shift in the universe we can't undo.

YOUNG MAN: And it's not just new, but different.

YOUNG WOMAN: I think the face masks *are* a unique addition. As well as—wait, has it started?

YOUNG MAN: I think it has—look, it's getting darker. And there are all those freaky half-moon shadows.

> *The small half-moon shadows have already begun to appear.*

YOUNG WOMAN: They're so cute! Like creepy little shadow smiles.

YOUNG MAN: But why are they smiles? It must be for a reason. Wait! They must hold a message for us—that's why they're smiles. That's where the truth always hides, behind your lips and teeth, buried deep underneath your tongue. They're the key. I'm sure.

YOUNG WOMAN: Let me listen. (*She gets up, bends down with her ear to the shadows, and listens.*) They say the time is getting closer. We need to be ready.

The next section builds up to overlapping in excitement.

YOUNG MAN: Do you think we'll get powers?

YOUNG WOMAN: Like flying?

YOUNG MAN: Or teleportation!

YOUNG WOMAN: A connection to the sun.

YOUNG MAN: And to the moon.

YOUNG WOMAN: I'll never be cold again.

YOUNG MAN: And I'll never overheat.

YOUNG WOMAN: We'll balance each other out perfectly.

YOUNG MAN: Just like the sun and moon.

YOUNG WOMAN: You can't have one without the other.

YOUNG MAN: That would be ludicrous.

YOUNG WOMAN: Absurd. (*Beat. She's brave and takes his hand, then looks straight ahead.*) They need each other.

YOUNG MAN: (*already certain, looking directly at her*) They need each other.

YOUNG WOMAN: (*looking right back at him*) They do. (*Beat.*) What if nothing happens?

YOUNG MAN: What do you mean?

YOUNG WOMAN: We've waited and dreamed and prepared for this moment, but what if it just passes us by? Or if we're not right?

YOUNG MAN: Of course it'll pass—that's what moments do. It's their job. And of course we're right—we're here together, aren't we?

YOUNG WOMAN: Well I want to stay here. In this moment. With you.

YOUNG MAN: Maybe that's one of the powers we'll get.

YOUNG WOMAN: Pausing time?

YOUNG MAN: (*searching*) The ability to live forever in a moment. A whole lifetime. Here, now.

YOUNG WOMAN: The two of us, here, together.

YOUNG MAN: I just want to be close to you.

YOUNG WOMAN: That's all I want too. Because change is hard. I like right now.

YOUNG MAN: The moon changes. The sun too. Everything, eventually.

YOUNG WOMAN: And that's precisely what we're waiting for. What everyone is waiting for. The great moment of change.

YOUNG MAN: That's it! That's what the message is. The change is coming.

YOUNG WOMAN: But I don't know if I want it, or if I can handle it.

YOUNG MAN: Well, maybe this is the great moment of change for *us* too. A song? A spell? A start?

YOUNG WOMAN: You mean the magic powers we're getting?

YOUNG MAN: In a way. But not adding something to us. Bringing out something that's already inside.

YOUNG WOMAN: What if it's not there? For me, I mean. You already have it, I know you do. But I've always felt stunted, short. Unable to break out of my own cycle, to fully be there, completely inhabiting myself.

YOUNG MAN: You're here now.

YOUNG WOMAN: Maybe.

YOUNG MAN: (*squeezing her hand*) You're you and you're here. I know you are.

YOUNG WOMAN: Hopefully.

Beat. They sit there in silence holding hands, pondering the universe/ each other (as each person is a universe in themselves, are they not?).

YOUNG MAN: It's almost time.

He stands up, extends his hand to her. She takes it, standing. They put their arms around each other, and sway back and forth to the music, a slow gentle togetherness. The stage grows darker and darker as they dance.

YOUNG WOMAN: Oh! We can't forget! (*She pulls out two pairs of solar eclipse viewing glasses.*) We need to be safe. For this to work.

YOUNG MAN: We do. We need to protect each other.

They put on the glasses. To anyone else they would look genuinely frightening—face masks and eclipse glasses. They appraise one another and realize they've never been more beautiful. It's silly and sweet and completely unique to their little moment of forever.

YOUNG MAN: I . . . see you.

YOUNG WOMAN: I see you too.

And they do. It is an overwhelming realization, to see and be seen so clearly. There's a word for it. A tear or two might roll down their cheeks, merging stickily with the face masks.

YOUNG WOMAN: I'm ready.

YOUNG MAN: Me too.

They hold hands again, strong in the face of what's to come. They stand and stare up into the sky as the solar eclipse reaches totality. Right as the final sliver of light hits their faces . . .

YOUNG WOMAN and YOUNG MAN: (*whispering at the same time to the sun, moon, and each other*) Thank you.

Slow fade to silence and blackout.

MAGGIE LEE (she/her) is a Seattle playwright who creates imaginative worlds on stage in genres like science fiction, fantasy, and horror, with productions in Seattle, New York, Seoul, Minneapolis, and San Francisco. In 2022, she was a contributing book writer for The 5th Avenue Theatre's original musical *And So That Happened*. Other productions include *Sheathed* (2019 Gregory Award Winner for Outstanding New Play), *The Flight Before Xmas*, *A Hand of Talons*, *The Tumbleweed Zephyr* (2016 Gregory Award Nominee for Outstanding New Play), and *The Clockwork Professor*. She was a Hedgebrook writer-in-residence (2021), a Jack Straw Artist Support Program residency awardee (2021), and the Resident Playwright at Macha Theatre Works (2020–2023). She is a Resident Playwright at Seattle Public Theater, a board member of Rain City Projects, a contributing writer for The Ugly Radio podcast, and a member of the Dramatists Guild. Her plays are available on New Play Exchange and published by Mneme Press.

Maggie Lee

Living Donor

CHARACTERS:

BRENDA   Female, a patient

PETER   Male, Brenda's brother

CASSIDY   Any gender, a TV reporter

MELANIE   Female, a kidney donor

SETTING:

A hospital room, present day.

BRENDA is lying in bed, dressed a hospital gown and prepped for surgery. PETER, her brother, anxiously fusses around her.

PETER: It's cold in here. Isn't it cold? Do you need a blanket? I can go get you a blanket. Or how about a drink of water, are you thirsty? Oh, right, you're not supposed to be drinking anything before the surgery. Sorry, I didn't mean to remind you. Now you're probably even more thirsty. Great, now I'm thirsty.

BRENDA: Peter, stop it. You're freaking out.

PETER: Sorry. I'm just nervous.

BRENDA: Why are you nervous? I'm the one who's going to get cut open!

PETER: I know, I know. It's stupid.

BRENDA: You always do this. Even when we were kids, I never got a chance to freak out about anything, because you were always freaking out enough for the both of us.

PETER: And look at what a fine, well-adjusted adult you turned out to be. Mom and Dad would have been so proud.

BRENDA: Yeah.

PETER: Look, I just wanted to say . . . I'm sorry.

BRENDA: Why?

PETER: I'm your only brother! The kidney should have come from me. I failed you. I'm a failure.

BRENDA: Don't be stupid. It's not your fault you have a different blood type.

PETER: But I should have . . . you know . . .

BRENDA: What? Forced yourself to grow different blood?

PETER: Yes?

BRENDA: Seriously?

PETER: Seriously, I totally would have given you mine in a heartbeat if I could. You know that, right?

BRENDA: I know.

PETER: Or any of my other body parts. My corneas are still good, I bet you could have one of those. I don't think they're as picky with eyeball stuff.

BRENDA: Peter! Listen. I love you, but you're crazy and you need to stop freaking out.

PETER: Fine. (*beat*) You really aren't cold? I'm freezing!

BRENDA: Okay! Would you please go get me a blanket?

PETER: Yes! Sure! Be right back.

> *PETER exits. A beat where BRENDA is alone, and she allows herself a tiny moment of freaking out. CASSIDY, a perky TV reporter, enters. They have an unseen camera operator with them.*

CASSIDY: Knock knock! Is this a bad time?

BRENDA: Uh, kind of. Who are you?

CASSIDY: Cassidy Winters, from Channel 10 News? Just stopped by to do a little interview before your surgery. We spoke with your doctors, and they said it was okay if we popped in to shoot a quick segment for the evening newscast.

BRENDA: Um, really? I mean, my ass is practically hanging out of this gown.

CASSIDY: Oh, no worries! We'll only shoot the front half. Our viewers love heartwarming stories like this. We get so many likes and nice comments on Facebook. You'll get such a kick out of it.

BRENDA: Actually, I don't really—

CASSIDY: Great! We'll be out of your hair in two shakes of a lamb's tail.

> *They gesture the unseen camera operator toward the audience.*

CASSIDY: Just set the camera up here. (*to BRENDA*) There's no need to worry about a thing, you look fabulous. Just look right over there and act natural.

BRENDA: There is nothing natural about this in the least.

CASSIDY: (*laughs*) You have such a great sense of humor! (*suddenly serious, out to the audience*) Okay, on me in 3-2-1 . . . I'm here at Mercy General with an amazing story of human connection. Brenda Song was just a humble receptionist working at the front desk of a downtown PR firm. Little did she know that her menial job would literally save her life. Brenda, what are your thoughts on that?

BRENDA: Um, yeah. I'm very grateful. But that wasn't exactly how—

CASSIDY: You see, when word got out that Brenda needed a kidney, she had to look no further than right down the hall for a savior. The Vice President of the company herself stepped up, eager to help a fellow co-worker in need, no matter how lowly the position. What a heartwarming story of solidarity in this modern day and age, isn't that right, Brenda?

BRENDA: I guess? Wait, did you just say "lowly"?

MELANIE enters, rolling an IV drip and clutching the backside of her hospital gown closed.

MELANIE: Brenda? Are you in here?

CASSIDY: And if it isn't the hero of the moment herself, Melanie Greene! It's so wonderful to meet you! Are you here to wish Brenda good luck before the surgery? Why don't you two hug, that would be such a great shot! Do you have anything to tell the folks at home?

MELANIE: No comment.

CASSIDY: But it's such a generous, selfless thing you're doing! Surely you'll want to inspire our viewers with your incredible story of courage and compassion?

MELANIE: Actually, I don't give a rat's ass about your viewers. Now take your little circus someplace else.

CASSIDY: I see.

They motion to the camera operator to cut the feed.

CASSIDY: We got enough footage, anyhow. (*smiles sweetly*) Thanks so much for your time, Brenda. And good luck with your new kidney.

CASSIDY exits.

BRENDA: Thanks.

MELANIE: Don't mention it. Those parasites can scrounge somewhere else for their feel-good fluff.

BRENDA: No, I mean, thanks. For everything.

MELANIE: Oh, that. It's nothing.

BRENDA: But it isn't nothing. It's like, my life. You're giving me my life. I don't know how I can ever repay you.

MELANIE: Don't be so dramatic, please. It's just a kidney. A piece of meat. It's no big deal.

BRENDA: Sorry, it's just . . . now that we're really going to do this, I have to ask. Why me? We aren't friends. I've worked in that office for five years and we've probably only said a dozen words to each other. I can't figure it out. Why would you do this for me?

MELANIE: Because it's not for you.

BRENDA: What do you mean?

MELANIE: Look, you have to understand something about me. I'm not nice, okay? The reason we've never talked is because I never talk to the receptionists. I don't want to waste my time or yours by pretending to be interested in what movies we saw or what we did over the weekend. I'm too busy and so are you. Work should just be about work.

BRENDA: I see. So . . . you don't have time to chit chat, but you do have time for major surgery?

MELANIE: Like I said, because it's not for you. It's because of my brother.

BRENDA: Your brother?

MELANIE: Yeah. He's sick. He needs a kidney.

BRENDA: I'm so sorry. You aren't a match? That must be so hard.

MELANIE: No, you don't understand. I have Type O blood, I'm a match for everyone. I'm giving you my kidney because it's the only way I don't have to give it to him.

BRENDA: Oh. (*realizing*) *Oh.*

MELANIE: You know how, even if you don't get along with your family all the time, there's always that one shining memory together that's pure and magical and fun? Like your birthday, or a perfect summer day at the beach, or the time they taught you to fly a kite or tie your shoe. Something honest and special that makes you remember why you love them?

BRENDA: Yeah?

MELANIE: Yeah. We don't have that. My brother is a terrible person. He's always been a terrible person. He sucks people dry until he has no more use for them, and then tosses them away like garbage. But I knew once it got out that he needed a kidney, I would have to step up. He'd be sure to raise a stink about it, and it wouldn't look good for me to have that out in the open. Professionally, you know.

BRENDA: So lucky me, I came along.

MELANIE: I remember all the whispering in the office when you got sick, people were really upset. And there were all these cards pinned on the wall behind your desk, like real handwritten notes saying nice things. And even though we never talked, you always looked up and smiled at me every morning, even though I'm sure most of those mornings you had nothing to smile about.

BRENDA: What can I say, it's my job.

MELANIE: So I thought, it's only a piece of meat, but it's my piece of meat. I don't care what the world says about who I owe it to, it's mine to give away. And at least you smiled at me, which is more than my brother ever did for our whole lives together. So . . . I'm doing this for me, and for me alone. I just wanted to tell you now, so that you don't have to be grateful afterward.

BRENDA: I understand.

MELANIE: Good. I'd better get back to my room. Good luck in there.

BRENDA: You too.

> *MELANIE nods curtly to her and exits. A beat. PETER enters with a blanket.*

PETER: This whole hospital is filled with beds, you'd think I wouldn't have to go all the way to Timbuktu to find one stupid blanket. What's wrong? Are you crying?

BRENDA: (*crying*) No.

PETER: I thought you said no freaking out! And then the minute I leave the room, you start freaking out?

BRENDA: I'm just cold. Can I have the blanket?

PETER: Sure.

> *PETER wraps the blanket around BRENDA and hugs her. They stay that way for a moment.*

PETER: What about your feet, do you need some thicker socks? Because I'm wearing some really comfy wool ones, I could just take them off and they'd already be warm and—

BRENDA: Just shut up, okay? (*beat*) And I don't want your lousy corneas either.

PETER: Okay. Whatever you say.

> *END OF PLAY*

BARBARA LINDSAY My first full-length play, *FREE*, won the NY Drama League's 1989 Playwrighting Competition and was given its premiere production in London in 1991. Since then there have been more than 400 national and international productions of my plays and monologues in 35 States, 13 countries, and on every continent except Antarctica. Full-length play *I-2195* won the Women in the Arts Award at UM St. Louis and was produced there in 2005. Short play *Here to Serve You* won the 2008 Goshen Peace Play Prize. One act *Heavenly Light* won the same prize in 2020. In 2011 I was Playwright-in-Residence for New Voices for the Theater, a two-week playwriting intensive for teens produced annually by SPARC (School of the Performing Arts in the Richmond Community) in VA. I am a fifth generation Californian living in Seattle, WA, married to an amazing man, and ridiculously happy.

Barbara Lindsay

Holy Hell

CHARACTERS:

THE MAN   a former asshole, 40's–50's

THE WOMAN   a former mother, 30's–40's

SETTING:

The play takes place whenever, wherever. A limbo set works best.
The two characters are in separate spaces and do not interact until
the last moment.

NOTES:

When this piece is played for tragedy and sorrow only, it becomes
unbearably dreary. Both characters must take a journey during the
course of the play, ending at a different emotional place from where
they started, and different from one another. THE MAN begins with
bravado, casually tough, almost proud of his exploits. His trajectory
is toward the opening of his heart, when he allows himself at last to
feel regret, to feel shame, to feel love. THE WOMAN begins in the
dark place of loss and despair. Her trajectory is toward quiet joy, the
happiness of loving and being loved, of being safe. The characters can
be of any ethnicity.

LIGHTS UP

THE MAN: Here's the thing about being an asshole, the main thing, maybe the only thing. You never look back. No matter what. You grab the purse off some old lady's shoulder, you don't look back to see did she have a heart attack or something, fall down, break a hip. No, you run, take the money, toss the purse, run some more. You jump a guy, smash his face in for no reason, you don't step back and think, "Now, did I maybe go too far? Like maybe this guy has a family to support?" No. You kick him when he's down, and then you run. But you definitely do not look back. You know, I was a kid once. Prob'ly okay, but who remembers? Some people grow up to be carpenters. I grew up to be an asshole. A petty asshole. Always running, like maybe I got a future to get to. Which I didn't.

THE WOMAN: I can remember my life before, although I don't think about it much. One moment it was just—life. Not very special, but good. And expected. And then suddenly one day, everything disintegrated. There were police and the money was gone, my husband was gone, and nothing was left but disgrace, and confusion. My father died soon after that and there didn't seem to be anything to keep me there any more. So I got a job, in California. I do remember, I remember clearly putting Toddy and Leesha into the car and starting toward our new life. I was excited at first, but it was a long drive, it seemed to go on forever. Maybe it was too long to take with two small children. I don't know. I don't remember the accident at all. No one knows what happened. Only that I drove off the road. I may have . . . I might have fallen asleep.

THE MAN: So this one day, I'm driving along, tossing some back, Jimi Hendrix turned up loud. And I pitch a bottle half full out the window, really let fly. And the thing you have to understand is, I meant no harm to nobody. This one time, I swear to god, I did not mean to fuck anybody up. Just tossing a bottle out the window. Littering at worst. But it must have hit this car I didn't see was there, 'cause suddenly behind me I hear tires skidding and a crashing sound, this car going out of control and flipping over. And I can't tell you, I cannot tell you why, but I did it. I did that one thing. I shoulda been disappearing like a puff of smoke, but, I don't know, I guess it caught me by surprise or something. It's crazy. A mystery to this day why I woulda done it. But I did. I looked back.

THE WOMAN: The first thing I remember is opening my eyes in the hospital. The room was very quiet, almost dark. Somebody was there next to the bed, a man I didn't know. He was holding my hand. Or I was holding his. I couldn't talk for a while, couldn't stay awake. The nurses and doctors came and went, but he always seemed to be there. I heard someone say that he had been the one to find us after the accident. And when I was able to ask about Toddy and Leesha, he was the one who told me they were dead. I can't imagine how he had the courage to tell me, and then to stay with me as I fell apart. My children . . . My children were gone. I had killed them. I believe I had to be strapped down for a long time. All I wanted was to slip away. I couldn't stand the thought that I might have to look anyone in the face, ever. But still he held on, he kept pulling me back to the surface for air. And when I looked at him, his face was so sad, as though he could feel everything I was feeling, and understood, and forgave me. How could anybody be that strong? Who was he? Why wouldn't he let me go?

THE MAN: I run back to look at the car. It was smashed pretty good, and the driver and these two little . . . Okay. So . . . I couldn't see much. One of them, one of them had red shoes. I couldn't tell if it was a boy or a girl, but . . . Holy mother, I wanted out of there, I was this close to skipping. Only then the driver, this lady, opened her eyes. I don't know if she saw me. But she looked right at me. So, anyway, I start flagging people down, got a guy with a cell phone, cops show up, ambulances, you know, the whole scene. And I'm practically standing there with my hands out, waiting to be cuffed, but everyone's all over these hurt people, and when the cops ask me what happened, I say I don't know— and they believe me! I had to've stunk of beer, but they treat me like some kind of hero just because I flagged somebody down. If they'da chased me, I'da run, but nobody chases, so I stand there like a fucking moron until they go to the hospital. That's when I coulda run. Nobody thought I was involved. But I knew. I'd seen what I'd done, you see? So I went to the hospital, too. I think maybe I'm praying to get nabbed or something, because the sight of those kids on the stretchers . . . I think, I *want* to pay. Some things you just shouldn't get away with. If I'da left, I'da had to drive off a bridge.

THE WOMAN: When I was released from the hospital, I couldn't even think about where I would go. There was nothing for me. Everything I had ever cared about was gone. He had walked me outside and he led me to the parking lot, and opened his car door. Just like that. As natural as air. You can't imagine . . . Without thinking, I put my hand on his cheek, and I kissed him. And right there, right in the parking lot, he sat on the ground and cried, just like a little boy. I think he is someone who had not felt loved before. It made me so happy. I'd been burdened with thinking I had nothing to give him in return, and now I knew. I could love him. And so I did. And so I do. I will love him for the rest of my life, no matter what.

THE MAN: I sat there in the lady's hospital room, waiting every second for the cops to come in. And when she comes to and she asks what happened to her kids, then I knew. The cops aren't going to take me away. No. I'm not going to jail. I get to do this instead. I get to look into this mother's eyes and tell her straight out that her kids are dead, and I did it. So I tell her. "They're dead," I say. And she puts her arms around my neck and holds onto me like I'm some kind of comfort or something. I mean, what the hell is this? "I'm an asshole!" I tell her. "I killed your kids! I almost killed you! You'll never have kids again and it's my fault! What the hell you doing?" But I guess I didn't say it so she could hear. I shoulda. I know I shoulda. I wish I could. We been together now ever since.

THE WOMAN: There has never been a gentler man. Never, not once, has he spoken a single harsh word to me. Not when the troubles of the world seem to rest on his shoulders, not when he's working day and night to pay the medical bills and make a home for us, not when I push him away because I'm too ashamed to let him look at me. I think he's my guardian angel. Isn't that funny? It's a silly idea, I know, and I feel foolish saying it. But so much bad happened, I find myself believing that God sent him to protect me. How else can I understand this? He's like all the goodness in the world wrapped up as a gift. And somehow, even though I don't deserve it, my name is on the tag and the gift is mine.

THE MAN: Every morning I wake up before her and watch her sleep, thinking, "Today is the day she's going to remember. Today is the day she'll look at me and know what I did." And every day she wakes up and smiles at me, and puts her hand on my face. And I let her. Because this is worse than anything. Seeing her every day, knowing what I know, and her not having a clue and treating me like I've got a decent bone in my body, now this, this is something all the cops and courts and jails in all the world got no equal of. I have to tell her. I know I have to tell her. I love her so much. I mean, look at her.

HE turns to look at her.

THE WOMAN: Look at him.

SHE turns to look at him. They both turn back.

THE MAN: It's almost more than I can bear.

THE WOMAN: It's almost more than I can bear.

LIGHTS DOWN

THE END

WILLOW MCLAUGHLIN is a playwright and educator based in Burlington, Washington. She is a graduate of Western Washington University with a B.A. in English/Theatre Education and a Masters in Theatre. Willow has spent the last twenty years writing for all ages. In her spare time, she also raised two boys, taught middle school, ran a theatre arts program for youth, and worked on more community theatre productions than she can count. She currently works as a freelance script writer for Watchmojo.com and as a substitute teacher for public schools. Willow has one published TYA play, five full-length community theatre productions, and more than seventy youth productions for acting programs and public schools. Her work can be found on NPX: New Play Exchange.

Willow McLaughlin

Be Batman

CHARACTERS:

MAY   An experienced mom with four children.
She is laid back and easy going.

LEA   A new mom with just one child. She is hyper
aware of her daughter at all times.

SETTING:

A park playground. The only set piece on stage is a bench at the park.

May walks in with a bag full of snacks and toys. She is looking out at the audience, as if the playground is in that direction. She is calling to her son.

MAY: One hand on the ladder at all times. And don't pee off the top of the slide this time, OK? (*sits on the bench and reaches into her bag, trying to find something*) What, Buddy? You bet! Be Superman! (*Suddenly realizes what was just said. Quickly jumps up*) No! Not Superman! No flying off the top of the slide. Be Batman and take a secret slide down to the ground. Be Batman. (*to herself*) Always be Batman. Then, you can be a millionaire and support mama in her old age.

May sits down and starts digging in her bag. Lea enters. She's holding out a plastic cup with a straw.

LEA: Sweetie, do you want any more of your smoothie? Use your words. No frownie faces. Smoothie first, then fruit snacks. Honey, not the merry go round. It goes too fast.

Lea runs offstage.

MAY: Batman, have you seen the Bat Phone? Again? Seriously? No, keep playing. You and I are going to have a chat about that later. (*to herself*) Meanwhile, Bat Mom has no protective shield.

Lea reenters.

LEA: Both hands on the ladder, Sweetie.

Lea stands to one side. May and Lea glance at each other, and then catch each other's eye.

MAY: How old is she?

LEA: Four.

MAY: Mine too.

LEA: It's such a fun age.

MAY: Yeah, way better than thirteen.

LEA: Oh, do you have a thirteen year old?

MAY: Yep. And a nine year old. And a seven year old.

LEA: Four! Wow. I just have the one. She keeps me on my toes. I don't know how you do four.

MAY: Lots of coffee and lots of wine.

LEA: (*too distracted to hear May's answer*) Both hands, Sweetie! (*to May*) I'm sorry. What did you say?

MAY: I read instructional manuals. All the time.

LEA: Oh, I just got this book from a friend of mine. It's called *Raising Human Beings*. It's about how to cultivate a better parent-child relationship while also nurturing empathy, honesty, resilience, and independence. Have you read it?

MAY: No, I've been reading a lot of *A Series of Unfortunate Events*.

LEA: Is that a book on raising children?

MAY: So to speak.

> *May starts to look through her bag again. Lea moves towards the playground again and calls out.*

LEA: No pushing. Just ask him nicely to move out of the way. Well, if that little boy won't move then just come back down the ladder. You can do something else. (*back to May*) It just makes me crazy when parents let their kids completely take over the equipment.

MAY: (*half amused*) I always figured it's good practice for life. Sometimes kids need to work things out on their own.

LEA: Well, that little boy in the superhero cape won't let her get on the slide. I mean, who lets their kids out in public like that anyway. It's not Halloween.

> *May stands and walks towards the playground to call out to her son.*

MAY: Batman! I don't think she knows the secret password. Why don't you tell it to her and let her through. Batman helps people, remember?

> *May smiles at Lea and sits back down. There is an awkward silence.*

LEA: What was the password?

MAY: Please.

LEA: (*to her daughter*) Are you going to swing now, Honey? Hold on! Let me clean off the chains.

> *Lea grabs some wipes and exits.*

MAY: (*calling off to her son*) Batman doesn't eat dirt. Says me! Because Alfred told me. (*holding up a snack*) Did you want this? Last chance! (*May shrugs and starts to eat it*) Sure, you can fly on the swings. Of course. Mama always give the best big pushes.

> *May exits as Lea re-enters.*

LEA: Both hands on the chains, Sweetie.

> *May runs on.*

MAY: Fly, Little Man!

LEA: Is that safe?

MAY: Swinging on his stomach? He does it all the time. I'm not sure he's ever actually sat on a swing seat. I don't blame him. They're so uncomfortable.

LEA: I don't really remember. It's been a long time. (*to playground*) No standing! I said sit. 1 - 2-

> *They sit in silence for awhile. May digs around in her bag.*

LEA: Did you lose something?

MAY: No, I left my book at home, and Batman over there put my phone in Joker's briefcase to track him, so he can catch him later.

LEA: Joker?

MAY: My husband. It's a thing they do. Which sounds odd, but that sums up our life pretty much, so . . . Do you know what time it is?

LEA: Sorry. My phone got lost in the move, and I haven't had a chance to get a new one.

MAY: I just feel weird without my phone.

> *May looks through her bag some more.*

LEA: I try not to have mine out at the playground anyway. I've just heard so many stories about kids disappearing as soon as their parent looks away. Or get distracted.

MAY: (*looking up from her bag*) Right.

LEA: (*standing and calling out*) She's fine. She doesn't like to be pushed too high! What's your little boy's name?

MAY: He's only answering to Batman this week.

LEA: And you're letting him get away with that?

MAY: If you can be Batman, why wouldn't you be?

LEA: OK. (*calling out*) Um, Batman? Can you please not push her so high?

MAY: (*calling out*) She's good, Batman. Nice job!

> *Lea backs up reluctantly.*

MAY: So you just moved here?

LEA: Yes, last week. This is our first trip to the park. Um, I'm sorry, but should your little boy be climbing to the top of the swing set like that?

MAY: Probably not.

LEA: Are you going to tell him to get down?

MAY: No.

LEA: Why not?

MAY: If I yell at him to get down, he'll take me very literally and jump.

LEA: From up there?

MAY: But, if I don't say anything, he'll wave at me from the top and then climb right back down. (*waving*) See, here he comes.

LEA: (*to her daughter*) No, Sweetie, you can't climb up there. (*taking a step towards the playground*) I said no. Come down now. We'll leave and go home!

MAY: She probably wouldn't get all the way to the top. Mine's been climbing things since he was born. One time I found him on top of this—

LEA: (*not paying attention to May*) Just because that little boy is doing something dangerous, it doesn't mean it's OK for you to do it. (*small gasp*) Oh no. (*calling as she goes off*) Are you OK? I'm coming.

> *Lea runs off, but May just watches calmly. Lea comes back on almost immediately.*

MAY: Any blood?

LEA: No. She could have gotten really hurt.

MAY: Wood chips are remarkably soft. Especially if you land on your butt. I know from experience.

LEA: Well, she wouldn't have fallen if she hadn't been copying your son. That's the problem with letting children do whatever they want. They set a bad example for others.

MAY: (*standing*) Right.

LEA: I didn't actually mean to say that out loud.

MAY (*calling out*) Batman, two minutes

LEA: I'm sorry. I didn't mean to offend you.

MAY: It takes more than that to offend me. I have four boys.

> *Lea starts eating her daughter's fruit snacks.*

LEA: I'm a horrible person.

MAY: Yep. (*Lea looks up startled at May's agreement*) Only horrible people eat their kid's snacks.

LEA: (*realizing what she's done*) Oh, no. I didn't bring any other snacks. She's going to freak out.

MAY: Here, you can have one of mine. I have a year's worth of supplies in this bag.

> *May holds out a fruit snack bag.*

LEA: Oh, no thanks, they're not organic.

MAY: (*with a forced smile*) Have a great day.

> *May starts to leave.*

LEA: No, I'm sorry. That came out wrong. My daughter is allergic to everything. The organic ones are the only ones that she's doesn't have a reaction to.

MAY: Do you have allergies?

LEA: No.

MAY (*hands Lea the fruit snacks*) I like the ones shaped like strawberries. They taste like pink. See ya.

LEA: I'm sorry if I ruined your afternoon.

MAY: Really, It's not you. School gets out soon and my olders have soccer. (*Calling out to the playground*) C'mon Batman! The Bat-mobile's ready to roll!

> *Lea stands and crosses to May.*

LEA: (*in a rush*) Wait, wait. I'm going to feel horrible about this whole thing if I don't apologize. I've just been a mess the last couple of weeks, since we got here. I haven't had time to unpack, we're living out of boxes, and I can't concentrate on anything. I feel like I'm going insane, and we don't know anyone and my husband shipped out yesterday and won't be back for three months, and I just over-shared to a total stranger on the playground, but you just seem like you have everything together, and I feel like a wreck, and I'm sorry. I know you have to go.

MAY: It's all good. And honestly none of us have it all together. But, I really do have to run. (*May starts to walk off, but comes back*) OK, listen, we have soccer today, but are you free tomorrow afternoon? My thirteen year old could watch all of the kids and I could help you unpack a few boxes. (*Lea seems hesitant*) He's actually really good at watching littles, when he's not rolling his eyes that is.

LEA: That's so much trouble for you.

MAY: If you can help, you should.

LEA: Like Batman?

MAY: Always be Batman.

MAY: (*holding out her hand*) I'm May.

LEA: (*shaking it*) Lea.

MAY: Tomorrow?

LEA: That would be great. I could make dinner?

MAY: Perfect. But, be warned, you have no idea how much four boys can eat. Um, neither of us have phones right now, so why don't you write your address down on this.

May pulls something random out of her purse and hands to it to Lea with a pen.

LEA: I don't want to make you late.

MAY: It's fine. I'd hate to interrupt the flying lesson anyway. (*Lea starts to step forward as she looks out at the playground. May puts a hand on her arm to stop her.*) They'll really be OK. That merry go round doesn't actually go that fast. It just feels like it when you're four.

Lea fills out her address and hands the paper back to May.

LEA: She looks like she's having a blast.

MAY: (*calling out*) C'mon Batman. You can play with your new friend tomorrow. It's all planned out. What's your daughter's name?

LEA: Robin.

Lights Out

JULY MONDAY A dual U.S./U.K. Citizen, Ms. Monday is a writer living many personas between London and Key Peninsula, WA. Graduate of The Juilliard School Playwriting Program under Marsha Norman & Chris Durang.

July Monday

Thirty Story Masterpieces

CHARACTERS:

LORI

THOMAS

A high-rise apartment at East 70th and 3rd Avenue, Manhattan.
Sunset.

A young man, THOMAS, sits on a couch.
Behind him, a gigantic window revealing a tangle of skyscrapers.

An attractive older woman, LORI, approaches.
Aphex Twin "Tha" plays throughout:

LORI: I'm going to make myself a martini.

THOMAS: Cool.

LORI: You want a martini?

THOMAS: No thanks.

LORI: It's early enough. It's early enough for a martini. I don't usually have one this early. Sometime you have to. Sometimes it's early enough for a martini. I bought myself this shaker, you like this shaker?

THOMAS: Yeah.

LORI: Shiny. Silver. Shaker. Do you like this?

THOMAS: Mmm?

LORI: Is the music okay?

THOMAS: Yeah fine.

LORI: I do like the classics.

THOMAS: Nice home.

LORI: I do like this apartment. I ended up looking at a lot of apartments but decided on this one.

THOMAS: It's nice.

LORI: They showed me some apartments downtown. Too small. I need a doorman. I like a doorman. Did you give him your name?

THOMAS: Yes.

LORI: Next time give a different name.

THOMAS: Okay.

LORI: Not your real name. He probably thinks you're my boyfriend. He probably thinks we're lovers. That's funny. That would be funny. I commissioned this painting, you know.

THOMAS: Nn.

LORI: I met with the painter. I sat for the painter. We fought a little. I wanted it to look a certain way but I suppose sometimes you have to acquiesce to artistic imagination. Cigarette?

THOMAS: Yeah, sure.

LORI: You smoke?

THOMAS: Yeah, sometimes.

LORI: What would your mother say?

THOMAS: . . .

LORI: I'm kidding, go ahead.

THOMAS: Thanks.

LORI: When I was your age they tried to outlaw these you know?

THOMAS: Oh yeah?

LORI: Yes they—let me light that—they started banning smoking indoors until they needed tax. What's your brand?

THOMAS: I don't know.

LORI: You don't have a brand.

THOMAS: I don't smoke enough.

LORI: No, you take care of yourself, don't you?

THOMAS: Yes, ma'am.

LORI: I've been going to the gym. There's a gym on the basement floor. I use the machines. When I was younger I was a championship cross trainer. When I was your age. You weren't even born. Were you born by then? Don't answer. I don't want to know the answer to that. We're strangers, really. You smoke with a stranger but you don't give him your car keys. Here. Ashtray.

THOMAS: Thank you.

LORI: I'm going to order food. Would you like any food?

THOMAS: No thanks.

LORI: It's on me.

THOMAS: What kind of food?

LORI: Have you ever had fish?

THOMAS: No.

LORI: Let's order fish.

THOMAS: I think that's really expensive.

LORI: I can afford it.

THOMAS: That's really generous.

LORI: It's not every day I get a visit from someone like you. There's a clean river in Canada they get these from. Let me just tap that into this fucking thing. (*on touchscreen*) "Two slices of salmon add boiled potatoes." Okay, coming in thirty minutes.

THOMAS: Thank you.

LORI: This won't spoil your dinner will it? Your wife won't be upset?

THOMAS: I don't mind eating twice.

LORI: What do you usually have?

THOMAS: For dinner?

LORI: Yes.

THOMAS: Fake something. I've had a lot of fake potatoes are these real ones?

LORI: Mmm hmn.

THOMAS: Yeah I'm really excited.

LORI: Then have a drink with me.

THOMAS: Sure. Yeah.

LORI: There's a man. (*makes drink*) So where do you live?

THOMAS: In the compounds below Canal.

LORI: With your wife.

THOMAS: Yes.

LORI: How's the air quality?

THOMAS: It was pretty bad but they replaced the filters last year.

LORI: This building has its own purifier.

THOMAS: We're having a baby soon.

LORI: Yes your mother told me.

THOMAS: My wife's really worried.

LORI: What about?

THOMAS: Money. Life in general. *Being* alive.

LORI: Drink.

THOMAS: Thank you. So . . . just you here?

LORI: Yep. My husband had the money but he *pfft*!

THOMAS: Died.

LORI: Suicide.

THOMAS: Damn.

LORI: Not *intentional*. But he killed himself. Second apartment. Found him dead with all these drugs.

THOMAS: I'm sorry.

LORI: Not me. The maid.

THOMAS: Still.

LORI: The problem with money is that you can buy a lot of drugs. And like, *good drugs*. (*she pops two pills then drinks them down with wine.*)

THOMAS: And my mom and you are friends from like . . . ?

LORI: When we were younger.

THOMAS: Before I was born.

LORI: No I was around for the first couple years. Your mother and me were at the same college where she met your father? You were two when I moved away.

THOMAS: Uh huh. I like your shades.

LORI: Yes they keep out the sun.

THOMAS: . . .

LORI: Did that make you uncomfortable?

THOMAS: No.

LORI: Me talking about your mother.

THOMAS: No.

LORI: What are you looking at?

THOMAS: Just . . . buildings.

LORI: Yes I like only looking at buildings and sky. I sometimes imagine it's 1940. A lot of these buildings were here then. There weren't these Chinese skyscrapers everywhere I mean look at *that* one. A glowing red pagoda at the top? That's not even Chinese. Oh *my*, I could get arrested for even *talking* like this. But the smaller buildings, you see the ones about twenty stories down? These Thirty Story Masterpieces? Imagine living when it was just those. They must have seemed huge.

But now they're cottages. I could throw my garbage on them if my windows opened.

THOMAS: You can't even see the street from here.

LORI: Yes isn't it wonderful?

THOMAS: . . .

LORI: Have you been out?

THOMAS: Mmm?

LORI: Have you been outside?

THOMAS: Yes I go outside sometimes.

LORI: Why?

THOMAS: Just to see what it's like.

LORI: Isn't that bad for you?

THOMAS: You can go out for two or three hours and they say it's fine.

LORI: You've been reading different news than me. I haven't been outside in God I can't remember when.

THOMAS: It's the same. The trees have started dying but not like, they're still *there* and everything but they're all brown.

LORI: Are you scared?

THOMAS: No.

LORI: No Jesus I'm paralyzed by the whole thing.

THOMAS: Still have to live life I guess.

LORI: Well cheers to that. I mean my windows are sealed. I have UV protection from the sun. Yesterday I sat here and watched a flock of birds arch over that building. Fifty birds moving, just folding into themselves at once. You have really nice eyes.

THOMAS: Thank you.

LORI: . . .

THOMAS: Why did my mom want me to see you?

LORI: Isn't it clear?

THOMAS: I sort of understand.

LORI: Well we don't need to talk about it. How are things with your wife?

THOMAS: We're getting along I guess.

LORI: You could be doing a little better though.

THOMAS: Everyone is having a very difficult time being alive right now.

LORI: I am somewhat spared of that burden.

THOMAS: Yeah?

LORI: I don't have same problems as everyone else. This puts me in a unique position as a human being. I have to decide how to position my philanthropy.

THOMAS: . . .

LORI: Do you want to go to bed now?

THOMAS: Mmm hmm.

LORI: Here's a card here for you.

THOMAS: Thank you.

LORI: I'll always put the money in the card. The card is a gift to you. It's nothing else. Just a gift. If anyone asks.

THOMAS: Okay.

LORI: Five thousand and a transport pass. For now.

THOMAS: Sounds fair.

LORI: This will help start that family your wife wants.

She brings him close.

LORI: You look like your father. You're really sweet and I really like you.

She kisses him.

*Lights fade in the room
but linger for a moment
on the outline of skyscrapers
before blinking to black.*

BETH RAAS-BERGQUIST (she/her) has had many short plays produced via 14/48: The World's Quickest Theatre Festival, even shorter plays featured when she was part of the Seattle sketch comedy group Spontaneous Human Combustion, and plays of all lengths produced via Ghost Light Theatricals, where she served as Artistic Director for 15 years. As an erstwhile director and actor, she has worked with all the companies listed above as well as Live Girls! Theatre, The Seattle Fringe Festival, Theater Schmeater, and more. Beth also worked as a teaching artist at Seattle Children's Theatre, Youth Theatre Northwest, Seattle Public Theatre, and others, and as an arts administrator at On the Boards. She is a graduate of Bennington College, and lives in Seattle with her partner Allanah, daughter Svea, and dogs Bu''ons and Toggle.

Beth Raas-Bergquist

Josh's Real Funeral

CHARACTERS:

AMY   I I years old (can be played by an adult)

LINDSAY   I I years old (can be played by an adult)

JOSH   8 years old (can be played by an adult)

SETTING:

A sleepover; Amy's bedroom.

Lindsay and Amy doing sleepover things; nail painting or sharing a cigarette out the window, or whatever "sleepover things" means to you. Josh is covered in a heap of blankets.

LINDSAY: This sleepover is a little weird with your dead brother in the room.

AMY: Just pretend he isn't here.

LINDSAY: I'm trying, but.

AMY: Try harder.

A beat.

LINDSAY: So . . . um . . . who do you have a crush on right now?

AMY: I don't know. Who do you have a crush on?

LINDSAY: . . . I don't know.

AMY: You have a crush on Mike.

LINDSAY: I do not!

AMY: I saw the way you looked at him in science on Thursday.

LINDSAY: It was just 'cause he took my test tube.

AMY: It was 'cause you want to take his "test tube" in your mouth and . . .

LINDSAY: Shut up!

They giggle. A beat.

JOSH: It's hot under here. Can I come out?

LINDSAY: . . . Uh . . .

AMY: Just ignore him.

JOSH: This isn't very fun.

AMY: It's not supposed to be fun you idiot.

JOSH: You said I could play with you.

AMY: I said you could play if we played funeral. Your funeral.

JOSH: But I'm bored.

AMY: Well, being dead is boring.

LINDSAY: I mean technically we haven't had a real funeral yet.

JOSH: Yeah! All you did was bury me under these blankets.

AMY: The point is, I didn't want you to play, but mom said you had to.

JOSH: Is this like when I had to be the garbage can? And the wall?

AMY: Exactly.

LINDSAY: But still. We can't be playing funeral if we didn't have a real funeral.

AMY: Ugh, Lindsay! You're missing the point.

LINDSAY: Yeah, but.

AMY Fine! Josh, Come out.

He does. She points a finger gun at him. He "dies". She buries him again in the blankets.

AMY: You were murdered by the mafia and thrown into a deep hole in the middle of the night.

JOSH: So I just lie here? It's hot.

AMY: Duh, it's a hot hole, Josh, and the dead don't feel temperature, so shut up. (*A beat.*) So anyway . . . did you see Helen's outfit on Friday?

LINDSAY: I thought it was cute.

AMY: It was a jumpsuit covered in a fruit pattern.

LINDSAY: So?

AMY: It was a fruit suit. She was wearing a rhyme.

JOSH: Please can we play something else? It's hard to breathe under here.

AMY: Shut up Josh. You're dead.

LINDSAY: I mean, he isn't really dead, unless we have a real funeral.

AMY: Lindsay! God!

A beat.

AMY: So . . . have you gotten your period yet?

LINDSAY: Oh my god! No! No! Who even talks about that?

AMY: Ok, sorry.

LINDSAY: And in front of your brother. Oh my god.

JOSH: What's a period?

AMY: See, he doesn't even know.

A beat.

LINDSAY: Look, Amy, if we're going to play funeral, I think we should do it right. Have a real funeral.

AMY: We did do it right.

LINDSAY: No. Josh deserves better than a death by the mafia.

JOSH: Thank you.

AMY: UGH. Fine. What would be a REAL funeral, Lindsay?

A beat. Lindsay becomes strangely calm.

LINDSAY: I'm an expert on real funerals. (*Gently.*) Come here, Josh. Lie on the bed.

He does. She folds his hands as though he's in a coffin.

LINDSAY: This is your wake. And I am your mother. (*She cries, dramatically.*) My poor son. He was such a good kid. And when he died unexpectedly, we were all just . . . devastated. He is survived of course by his parents. And for the moment at least by his sister.

AMY: Oh, we're only playing funeral once. I'm not dying.

LINDSAY: We'll see. (*Cries dramatically again.*) Now, go on, honey, it's your turn.

AMY: Honey?! Am I supposed to be your husband?!

LINDSAY: I know it's hard to accept our Josh's death, but you need to live in reality now. Say a few words.

AMY: Um, Josh was a good son. We . . . um . . . played football together and did guy things.

JOSH: Guys can play with dolls and stuff too. Don't be sexist, Amy.

LINDSAY: Shhhh. Shhhh. You rest, corpse. You rest now. Honey, go on.

AMY: And we also played with dolls. And, um . . . he was a good son to me, his father. Uh . . . amen.

JOSH: Thank you.

LINDSAY: Shhhh. (*She caresses his face.*)

JOSH: Um . . . please don't touch my face?

LINDSAY: Shhhhh. (*She caresses his face again.*) Poor corpse led such a short life. He loved his football, and his dolls, and most of all, he loved to play with his sister, Amy. Didn't he?

AMY: Am I still your husband or am I me now?

LINDSAY: But Amy didn't want to play with him. Amy wanted him to pretend to be the wall. Or a garbage can. Or dead. Didn't she, corpse?

JOSH: Is my name corpse now?

LINDSAY: (*Again, with tenderness.*) The dead lose their names when they die.

JOSH: Could you stop touching my face?

LINDSAY: Shhhh. (*She does not stop touching his face.*) Everything to Amy is just so much furniture, isn't it, corpse? But death is peace.

JOSH: Um . . . yes?

LINDSAY: It doesn't have feelings. Or secrets. It doesn't want to talk about its period.

AMY: Lindsay, what the fuck?

JOSH: I mean, Amy, you do always make me be furniture. Or dead.

AMY: Because you always want to play with me when I have friends over. I have my own life!

JOSH: I know! But I don't have a friend over tonight.

AMY: Because you don't have friends!

JOSH: I do too!

LINDSAY: Corpse, you rest now. You lie die down now. Shhh. Shhh.

JOSH: I don't want to play anymore.

AMY: Lindsay, you're creeping me out.

LINDSAY: His sister said he didn't have friends. But Josh did have friends. He had his dream friends. He had Bunny and Chicken.

JOSH: I do miss my dream friends sometimes. Like when we found the trampolines.

AMY: And Bunny said,

JOSH: I wish we could hop together forever. And Chicken said,

AMY: Bawk bawk bawk bawk bawk!

JOSH: That's how me and Amy used to play. Before she made me be the trash can.

LINDSAY: Shhhh, Corpse. Shhhh.

JOSH: Amy, I can't move.

AMY: BAWK!

JOSH: Amy?! MOM? MOM!

LINDSAY: Shhhh. His sister tried to say something nice for once, but it was too late. It was already Josh's funeral. His real funeral.

AMY: Bawk bawk bawk bawk bawk!

LINDSAY: And poor, dear corpse always wondered . . .

AMY & JOSH: Why Bunny spoke like a person, but Chicken just spoke like a chicken.

AMY: Bawk bawk bawk!

LINDSAY: But it doesn't matter now. Shhh, corpse, you sleep. You sleep, corpse.

Josh falls asleep. Amy is stuck as Chicken.

AMY: (*Trying to wake up Josh.*) Bawk?! Bawk bawk bawk! Bawk! Bawk!

LINDSAY: Maybe you shouldn't be such a bitch, Amy. Your brother loved you.

AMY: BAWK! BAWK! Bawk bawk bawk bawk!

LINDSAY: Shhhh. You sleep now Chicken. You sleep, corpse. It's time for your real funeral.

She lays Amy down on the floor. She covers her with the blankets originally used to bury JOSH, perhaps softly singing. Amy fights it at first, but slowly relaxes and falls asleep.

LINDSAY: Shhhhhhhh.

Blackout.

WAYNE RAWLEY's plays include *Christmastown: A Holiday Noir* (Seattle Public Theater), *Attack of the Killer Murder . . . Of Death!* (Seattle Public Theater, Theater Schmeater), and a multi-media adaptation of Orwell's *1984* (Empty Space Theater). His play *Live! From the Last Night of My Life* has been produced by Theater 22, and Theater Schmeater in Seattle, Sacred Fools in LA, The OU School of Drama, and was the winner of the 2012 Theater Puget Sound Gregory Award for Outstanding New Play. His play *Christmastown* was nominated for a 2015 Gregory Award. His short plays *Controlling Interest* and *The Scary Question* are published by both Vintage Press and Playscripts, Inc. and have seen hundreds of performances around the world. He is the creator of Seattle's late-night theater smash *Money & Run*, and wrote 9 episodes of the TV parody series, produced in Seattle, LA, and Berkeley. Wayne was the recipient of the 2010 Faith Broome Playwriting Residency at the University of Oklahoma. He is a teaching artist, working with young artists at ACT Theater, Seattle Public Theater, and Cornish College of the Arts, his alma mater. He lives in Seattle with his wife and two children.

Wayne Rawley

The Scary Question

CHARACTERS:

BRIAN   Linda's boyfriend

LINDA   Brian's girlfriend

SETTING:

Linda's living room couch.

NOTES:

A double asterisk (**) in a line means the person with the next line should begin speaking.

BRIAN and LINDA can be played members of any race, ethnicity, or gender. Names can be altered to sound appropriate and roles can be swapped between male and female genders to ft any cast a production would like.

AT RISE:

LINDA and BRIAN are sitting on the couch, LINDA at one end and BRIAN at the other. LINDA is reading some document for work. BRIAN is flipping through his own book or magazine. BRIAN is having trouble concentrating and looks nervously up at LINDA a couple times before speaking.

BRIAN: Question.

LINDA: Hm?

BRIAN: Question.

LINDA: What question.

BRIAN: For you.

LINDA: Question for me?

BRIAN: Yes.

LINDA: Are you okay?

BRIAN: (*defensive*) Yes!

LINDA: Okay.

BRIAN: I need to ask you a question.

LINDA: Okay.

BRIAN: How long have we been together?

LINDA: Eight months.

BRIAN: That's right!

LINDA: I know!

BRIAN: You like 'em?

LINDA: Huh?

BRIAN: You like 'em, the eight months?

LINDA: Of course.

BRIAN: Me too.

LINDA: Good.

BRIAN: Hell, yes it's good!

LINDA: Okay.

BRIAN: Okay.

> *They go back to reading.*

BRIAN: That's not the question.

LINDA: I'm supposed to read this for work.

BRIAN: I'm distracting you?

LINDA: No—

BRIAN: Because I don't want to distract you—

LINDA: No. That's okay. There is something on your mind. I want to know what it is.

BRIAN: I love you.

LINDA: I love you too.

BRIAN: When did we first say I love you?

LINDA: Um, four months ago.

BRIAN: Right!

LINDA: I know—

BRIAN: You knew!

LINDA: That's right.

BRIAN: Four months!

LINDA: You cried.

BRIAN: I was happy!

LINDA: So was I!

BRIAN: Okay!

LINDA: Okay.

BRIAN: Eight months, four months.

LINDA: I've never been happier.

BRIAN: Me either!

LINDA: Good.

BRIAN: Good does not begin to describe it.

LINDA: Okay.

BRIAN: Okay.

LINDA: Okay.

BRIAN: So—

LINDA: Honey, please just ask your question!

BRIAN: I'm sorry!

LINDA: What?

BRIAN: I just—

LINDA: What.

BRIAN: This isn't exactly easy—

LINDA: What isn't?

BRIAN: It's important, and I'm just not sure . . .

LINDA: Oh, my God. Brian. Stop it. Is it bad? You're scaring me.

BRIAN: It's scary. I'm scared to ask it—

LINDA: Brian, ask it!

BRIAN: Okay! So I'll just ask it. Then. Okay.

He gets down on one knee next to LINDA.

LINDA: Brian?

BRIAN: Linda, I wanted to ask you this for so long… What would you do if the Zombies attacked?

LINDA: What?

BRIAN: What would you do if Zombies attacked.

Pause.

LINDA: I'm sorry, **I don't know what you mean.

BRIAN: The Zombies. If they attacked. What would you do?

LINDA: What Zombies are you talking about?

BRIAN: Any Zombies—any and all Zombies. A horde of Zombies** from the cemetery, whatever—

LINDA: Horde of Zombies?

BRIAN: What I'm asking** is this—

LINDA: This is what** you wanted to ask me?

BRIAN: Should the proper set of circumstance align, be they atmospheric, environmental, chemical, industrial, viral, biological or supernatural that caused—

LINDA: That's weird, Brian, that is—

BRIAN: THAT caused the crazed, unholy and recently deceased to rise from the grave in search of succulent human flesh—

LINDA: Gross!

BRIAN: Yes. You're right. It is gross. Nevertheless—what would you do?

LINDA: Why are you asking me this?

BRIAN: Because it's important—

LINDA: No it isn't.

BRIAN: YES! It is!

LINDA: Why is it important?

BRIAN: Because I love you and you know what? I really do love you—and I want . . . I hope . . . that is to say, I'm ready for our relationship to . . . move. To the next level—

LINDA: You want to get married?

BRIAN: Whoa, wait a minute; you're asking me to marry you?

LINDA: I thought you were asking me to marry you!

BRIAN: I was asking about Zombies!

LINDA: Brian! What do you mean next level!

BRIAN: The next level! The level—above the current level!

LINDA: Moving in together?

BRIAN: Ah-hah—Well, okay, you know, I'm not sure. I'm afraid—

LINDA: Of Zombies?

BRIAN: Well, you didn't come to Zombie night.

LINDA: You're mad about Zombie night.

BRIAN: I'm not mad—

LINDA: You said it was okay that I didn't come to Zombie night!

BRIAN: It was—

LINDA: You said you didn't mind if I skipped Zombie night!

BRIAN: (*Finally, as if it has been bothering him for days*) Well, why would you want to skip Zombie night? It was awesome! We watched *Night of the Living Dead, Dawn of the Dead, Return of the Living Dead* and *Return of the Living Dead II*, which sucked I admit that, but *Return of the Living Dead* was awesome and why didn't you want to come?

LINDA: I don't like Zombie movies.

Pause.

BRIAN: Wha? **What do you—

LINDA: I don't like Zombie movies.

BRIAN: That doesn't register with me, that—

LINDA: I don't like **them.

BRIAN: That doesn't compute. **Don't like them?

LINDA: No, You're getting it right. I. Don't. Like. Zombie. Movies.

    Pause.

BRIAN: What?

LINDA: Brian, this is ridiculous

BRIAN: No, it is not! No it is not ridiculous!

LINDA: They are gratuitous.

BRIAN: It happens to be a very viable genre.

LINDA: They are disgusting.

BRIAN: They ARE quite often a very pointed and highly savvy commentary on the mindless consumerism of late 70's, early 80's Middle America.

LINDA: No they aren't!

BRIAN: Zombie Movies are my life!

LINDA: No they aren't!

BRIAN: No! That's not totally true, they aren't totally my life, but I love them! I love them Linda! I love them!

LINDA: Okay! Great! I'm glad you love them! Love them! I love modern dance!

BRIAN: That's not really dance. They're just hopping around, anyone can do that.

LINDA: See! See! I don't like Zombie movies, you don't like modern dance!

BRIAN: No! No! That's you—That's a diversion! That's you trying to create a diversion!

LINDA: You have lost your mind

BRIAN: It's true I have! I have lost my mind. When I wake up in the morning, the first thing I ask myself is 'I wonder if she is going to smile today,' and when I think that, I smile. And if I do some thing, in the day, that makes you smile? And you smile? And I see you smile? I die. Every time. Because, and I am being honest, I do not think there is anything more beautiful that has ever existed in the world than you smiling. All I want out of my life is to maybe see that most beautiful thing in the world just once a day. But, and I am also being honest—I have great fear about making it work with a woman that has no Zombie plan.

LINDA: A Zombie plan.

BRIAN: A small amount of thought given to a possible plan of escape should the dead rise from the grave and begin to walk the earth.

LINDA: Brian, I don't have a Zombie plan.

BRIAN: I know. I'm sorry. I've ruined everything. It's too soon—It's too—I'm sorry. I'll go.

LINDA: You're leaving?

BRIAN: I'm pushing you. I promised myself I wouldn't do that.

LINDA: Flamethrowers.

BRIAN: What?

LINDA: Do we get flamethrowers?

BRIAN: (*Sad. She just doesn't get it*) No. A flamethrower won't do us any good. They're Zombies. They're not gonna stop just because they're on fire. By the time they are burned enough to become incapacitated, they will already have eaten your brain.

LINDA: What about grenades?

BRIAN: Hand grenades?

LINDA: Yes.

BRIAN: No. The collateral damage would **be too massive.

LINDA: What does that mean? ** Like blowing up the house?

BRIAN: Like blowing up yourself, these Zombies **are like right outside—

LINDA: Okay. So what if I've got a flamethrower—

BRIAN: Linda, you can't—

LINDA: Listen, I've got a flamethrower, you grab the aluminum baseball bat out of the hall closet. You stand at the door—they're around the house right?

BRIAN: Completely surrounding the house and probably breaking through the barricades we've set up in front of the windows at this point.

LINDA: You stand at the door, I open the door for you and you run out swinging that bat at everything that moves. You clear a path to the car, because they're rotting, their heads come right off with one crack of the bat, so you clear a path to the car; we make it to the car. I jump in the back seat, you drive.

BRIAN: Keep talking.

LINDA: You start the car and speed off, screeching the tires with smoke coming off them and everything, I pop up through the sun roof with the flamethrower—they are all chasing us at this point right?

BRIAN: (*impressed*) Yeah. Yeah, they're chasing us all right.

LINDA: I pop up through the sunroof with the flamethrower and torch the bastards right back into the grave that spawned them. They'll never catch us 'cause we're in the car. And they aren't like superhuman or anything—

BRIAN: No, they aren't any stronger or faster than normal humans—

LINDA: Right, so they can't catch us, 'cause we're in the car and they are all on fire, running around bumping into each other setting each other on fire, burning up to incapacitation, and we escape. This time.

BRIAN: That could work.

LINDA: Then you and I find the resistance movement and join up.

BRIAN: Seriously?

LINDA: Yep.

BRIAN: You would join the resistance movement?

LINDA: The world is crawling with the living dead, Brian. We have to find the last bastion of humanity and align ourselves with them. Besides, if our species is going to survive, we are going to have to learn to work together.

BRIAN: Oh, my God. That is so true. I love you.

LINDA: I love you too.

They kiss.

BRIAN: Do you really want to live together?

LINDA: Of course. I can't wait. But we should. Wait. For months. I think.

BRIAN: Agreed. It's a big step. You are so right.

END OF PLAY

MATT SMITH writes often-absurd comedies about navigating a bruising world. His plays have been performed at schools and community theatres across the country, as well as the American High School Theatre Festival at Edinburgh Festival Fringe. Notable projects include *The Hanford Invasion!* (2018 Seven Devils New Play Foundry, 2022 finalist for the Woodward/Newman Award at Bloomington Playwrights Project); *Artist Retreat* (published by Pioneer Drama Service); and *The Last Quest of Visilock* (developed with Westlake High School's Performing Arts Department). More information at www.mattwritesplays.com.

Matt Smith

Doctor Loopifer's Machine

CHARACTERS:

SELMA   (F, any age) A suburban neighbor whose
                     hamster recently passed away.

VALERIE   (F, any age) Her suburban friend, stickler for
                     the home association's rules.

DOCTOR LOOPIFER (F, any age) An eccentric.

SETTING:

A suburban garage (garage door is open), with a large cardboard box in
the middle.

NOTES:

When talking as the hamster, *squeak* means making the squeaking-
type noises that a hamster might.

SELMA and VALERIE, two suburban neighbors, enter.

SELMA: Hello? Neighbor?

VALERIE: Doctor Loopifer?

SELMA: Are you sure that's her name?

VALERIE: One time I got her mail, and that's what it said. "Loopifer."

SELMA: It's so strange.

VALERIE: Everything about her is strange. She mows her lawn inconsistently. She hasn't joined the association's social hours. I've never even met her.

SELMA: Didn't you return her mail?

VALERIE: I just stuck it in her mailbox and ran away. The last thing I'm going to do if I'm curious about someone is talk to them.

SELMA: I saw her once, when I was out walking . . . you know, back when I took Bananas for walks.

VALERIE: Yeah, it was very strange you walked your hamster.

SELMA: Bananas loved it.

VALERIE: Well, now that she has passed, you can get a new pet. One that fits in the neighborhood better.

SELMA: I could never replace that magnificent hamster. Oh, just talking about her makes me tear up.

VALERIE: You have to stop dwelling on this. Have you tried brunch yoga?

SELMA: What's that?

VALERIE: It's light stretching followed by heavy food.

SELMA: I don't think that will help. The worst of it is I never got to say goodbye. I never should have let her out while the Roomba was on. Those electronic vacuums just don't know when to stop.

DOCTOR LOOPIFER, an eccentric, enters.

LOOPIFER: This is my garage. (*Taking a garage door clicker from her pocket.*) You are not invited. Begone. (*Clicking the garage door clicker. Nothing happens.*) This thing is malfunctioning, but imagine a garage door is slowly coming between us.

SELMA: Hi. I'm Selma, I live across the—

VALERIE: We both live in the neighborhood, and we require you to control the noise level emanating from your property.

LOOPIFER: Ridiculous. I am not aware of any noise.

> *Ominously, a loud, electric hum comes from the box.*

VALERIE: That. That's the noise.

SELMA: It woke us both up last night.

LOOPIFER: It's not my fault you choose to sleep at night.

VALERIE: That's a normal time to sleep.

LOOPIFER: Ack! Normal. I spit at normal. I am an inventor. I think outside the box.

VALERIE: (*re: the box in the garage*) What's that?

LOOPIFER: That's a box I invented.

SELMA: Tell us what it does.

LOOPIFER: (*annoyed*) I can't do that.

SELMA: Then make sure it's quiet.

LOOPIFER: (*very annoyed*) I can't do that either.

SELMA: Then we will call the police.

LOOPIFER: (*not annoyed at all*) Whoa. Whoa. Let's calm down.

SELMA: Yeah, we got your attention, don't we?

LOOPIFER: We don't need to get the police involved. My work requires a lot of chemicals that may not be . . . properly zoned. Maybe we can arrange a deal. Have you ever lost someone close to you?

SELMA: What?

LOOPIFER: What if you could talk to them one last time.

SELMA: I don't understand.

LOOPIFER: Behold!

> *LOOPIFER turns the box around and reveals a label on it that says "The Séance Machine."*

VALERIE: The Séance Machine?

LOOPIFER: This harnesses spiritual energy to create a portal between this world and the next. Mwhaahahahahaha!

VALERIE: You labeled it with a Sharpie.

LOOPIFER: There's a lot of boxes in the garage. I don't want to mix up a portal to the dead with my Christmas decorations.

SELMA: You could talk to anyone?

LOOPIFER: Yes.

VALERIE: You're not buying this, are you?

SELMA: It's interesting.

VALERIE: It is not interesting. It's a hazard. Now, the association requires—

SELMA: Wait. (*To LOOPIFER*) If it works, I won't call the police.

VALERIE: Selma.

SELMA: If it doesn't work, then we call them. Okay?

> *VALERIE considers and is okay with it.*

LOOPIFER: Okay, but you must do what I say. This is a precise, scientific instrument. Now let's all hold hands. (*They hold hands.*) Mmmmmm. Come on, it doesn't work if you don't moan.

VALERIE and SELMA: Mmmmmmm.

LOOPIFER: Mmmmmmmmm. (*Chanting*) And now. We focus our energy on the one we name:

SELMA: Bananas.

LOOPIFER: Bananas? You miss your breakfast?

VALERIE: Her hamster.

LOOPIFER: Oh. Okay then. Bananas.

SELMA and LOOPIFER: Bananas. Bananas.

VALERIE: Neighbors are going to see us over here and this is crazy. You cannot bring the spirit of a hamster. I don't think hamsters even have spirits, they're just bigger mice. And another thing—

> *Large electric hum as before. Now VALERIE is possessed by the spirit of BANANAS.*

VALERIE: *Squeak?*

SELMA: Bananas?

VALERIE: *Squeak!*

LOOPIFER: This is unprecedented in my scientific work. Not just communion but full scale possession!

> *LOOPIFER takes out a notebook and begins documenting everything.*

SELMA: How you doing girl?

VALERIE: (*confused*) *Squeak.*

SELMA: You're back.

VALERIE takes a step forward and almost falls down. She gets used to this new body.

SELMA: Do you miss me?

VALERIE: Yes.

SELMA: Did you say . . .

VALERIE: Yes.

SELMA: You can speak!

VALERIE: I finally have vocal muscles to speak. To say what I always wanted to say: I. Love. Cardboard.

SELMA: Bananas loved cardboard.

VALERIE: Do you have some? Maybe the center of a roll of paper towels?

SELMA: Oh, I have missed you so much. You completely understand me.

VALERIE: *Squeak.* That's the hamster word for "love."

VALERIE and SELMA embrace.

LOOPIFER: Bananas, you have been in the next plane of existence. Describe it for posterity.

VALERIE: Oh, there's a lot of tubes. Some for running through. And some for chewing.

SELMA: It sounds nice.

VALERIE: It's great and—oh! Who's that? *Squeak!* (*As VALERIE*) Selma! I'm trapped in my own body!

SELMA: What's happening?

LOOPIFER: Alas, it appears one body is not designed for two souls.

SELMA: No! Can't Bananas stay?

LOOPIFER: If she did so, the other soul would drop into the void.

VALERIE: (*as VALERIE*) A void? I don't want that.

LOOPIFER: (*to SELMA*) I'm sorry. You have to choose between your hamster, or your friend.

SELMA: I mean, I wouldn't say friends. We're neighbors.

VALERIE: (*as VALERIE*) Selma!

SELMA: Oh all right. Let me just say goodbye.

VALERIE: (*as VALERIE*) Fine. (*As BANANAS*) *Squeak.* I think I have to go back.

SELMA: Yes. You have to run in your ball all over the underworld. We will be apart, but I'll go on. I'll get a normal pet, and learn brunch yoga, and find my true home in all these association homes that look exactly alike. Oh that sounds so boring. (*To LOOPIFER*) Can I go with Bananas?

LOOPIFER: Well, that means you would die.

SELMA: (*to BANANAS*) It's a place with plenty of tubes?

VALERIE: (*as BANANAS*) *Squeak.*

SELMA: That's fine by me.

> *SELMA gets in the box. She lowers herself in, while maintaining eye contact with BANANAS.*

SELMA: Let's go home.

VALERIE: (*as BANANAS*) Sing to me. My favorite song.

SELMA: (*as she descends, she sings BANANAS' favorite song, to the tune of "Na Na Hey Hey Kiss Him Goodbye."*) Ba-na-na-na. Ba-na-na-na. Hey hey hey. Goodbye.

VALERIE and SELMA: Ba-na-na-na. Ba-na-na-na. Hey hey hey.

SELMA: Good-bye.

> *SELMA disappears from view. The loud electric hum again. VALERIE shakes as she reclaims her body.*

VALERIE: Oh my goodness! Selma! (*Grabbing into the box, pulling out SELMA's arm. It is limp. VALERIE lets go, terrified.*) What have you done? I am telling the association!

> *VALERIE exits in horror.*

LOOPIFER: And that is why I'm a cat person.

> *Blackout. End of play.*

OZZY WAGNER is an emerging playwright and librettist from Seattle, now based in NYC. They received a BA in Playwriting from Emory University, where they produced the student playwriting festival and received the Lucius Lamar McMullan award for extraordinary promise. Ozzy's work, often experimental, has been invited to festivals such as KCACTF (2020, 2021), Essential Theater's Bare Essentials readings, Barter Theater CPF, Horizon Theater's NSYPF, Theater Emory's Viral Plays, etc.; and has been developed through Seattle Opera's 23/24 Jane Lang Davis Creation Lab, The Workshop Theater, and Silver Glass Productions' Experimental Playwriting Workshop. @ozzy.writes

Ozzy Wagner

Don't Feed Dead Roses your Drinking Water

CHARACTERS:

ALICE

GEO

SETTING:

(In and around) a kitchen

NOTES:

TW: abuse, mentions of self harm

Milk the pauses as much as the lines;

the script lends itself to intentional scene changes with a minimal set.

In case there is any doubt: Alice is not losing her mind.

I.

A crackled record plays "You're Laughing at Me," Ella Fitzgerald.

ALICE: "Why do you think it's funny when I say that I love you soooo"

The door slams open. Lights—a bouquet of roses sits on the kitchen counter, in a vase.

ALICE: (*turning off the record player.*)
   . . . Hi.

GEO: Hi!

ALICE: What are you doing in my house?

GEO: I've come to rescue you.

ALICE: How romantic. From what?

GEO: Life!
   Liberty!
   The pursuit of happiness!

ALICE: Okay; My love. My light.
   I *did* tell you I have work today, didn't I?

GEO: You're taking a sick day.

ALICE: Am I!

GEO: I am getting you OUT of this house, and we are going *dancing*.

ALICE: Why do you sound so scripted?

   Beat.

GEO:

   -

   May I have this dance?

   She takes his arm. Lights. Ella.

II.

   ALICE's kitchen is full of flowers. The roses hang above the sink.
   She pours water in a bowl or wine glass and drinks it.
   Fade. A vase cracks.

III.

Lights again. ALICE cleans broken glass from the ground. She has a phone to her ear. At some point, she cuts herself on the glass.

ALICE: nothing's wrong.

-

-

-

I'm just

-

so thirsty all the time

-

-

-

Oh, no
He's great
He's wonderful

-

-

-

-

(*of the broken glass:*)
Can I recycle this?

VI.

ALICE is alone with the flowers, now hanging above the sink. She gulps.

She pours herself a cup of water, then looks at the vase; sometimes lies fill empty spaces.

She picks it up; it still has some flower water left in the very bottom.

She brings it to her nose—bad idea.

She washes it. Once for the grime, then twice. A third, for good measure.

She takes down the roses. Sometimes lies fill empty spaces—sometimes we do it ourselves.

She arranges them in the vase. A moment. She remembers her cup.

She feeds the dead roses her drinking water and pretends the vase is full.

VII.

GEO and ALICE. ALICE holds out a bouquet of flowers.

ALICE: Viscarias.

GEO: Oh.

ALICE: (*a confession*) I googled it.

GEO: Thank you.

He takes them, then sets them on the counter.

ALICE: Already cut the tips off. So you don't have to.

GEO: Oh.

ALICE: Cut my hands a little. So you don't have to.

He pulls down a drinking glass.

ALICE: Be careful
Your hands

He puts them in the glass. He doesn't fill it.

ALICE: . . . Do you like them?

GEO: (*not mean*)
You're anxious.

-

Don't be.

GEO kisses her, handing her one of the flowers, and exits.

ALICE sits on stage, looking at it.

GEO hasn't exited fully. His back to the audience, he takes the vase and lifts it,

very, very slowly, above his head. We're not sure what he's doing; he's not close enough to hit her.

She does not see him. They do not see each other.

This should continue, the looking and the raising, for a full minute.

She eats the flower.

VIII.

A strange humming goes on for a while. It stops. A vase shatters. It begins again.

When the lights return, there is a whole line of filled drinking glasses on the counters, each dedicated to one, very dead flower. We watch for long enough that we feel as though we've begun to watch a new show with an all-floral cast. ALICE breaks from the humming, but we can't make out what she's saying just yet. She repeats something, over and over. We never find out what it is.

IX.

In the darkness, GEO sings.

GEO: "You've got me worried and I'm all at sea; for while I'm crying for you, you're—"

The door slams open. Lights.

Kitchen again. Their kitchen. There are dishes in the sink. The vase is in a cupboard somewhere; sometimes we hide lies in hard-to-see places.

ALICE: Hi!

GEO: Um. Hi.
What are you doing home?

ALICE: I've come to rescue you.

Beat.

GEO: Don't you have work?

ALICE: Yes.

GEO begins to exit.

ALICE: Please dance with me.

A vase shatters.

X.

Ella plays, again.

Beat. Lights. GEO, again, with the vase. ALICE flinches, but he doesn't hit her. Instead, he pours it on the ground. She reaches for the water, desperately—

Blackout.

XI.

Darkness.

ALL:

I wish he would hit me
I wish he would hit me
I wish he would hit me
Can I ask him to?
I think he might understand
I think it might be simpler

XII.

ALICE sees us. Is she going to ask us to hit her?

The dead flowers are in a pile downstage. Maybe ALICE gathers more.

They seem to come from everywhere.

ALICE:

Did you know I kept them?
I'd pin them to my walls
Put them in little jewelry boxes
Press them in books between starbucks napkins
It was weeks before I stopped finding their hiding places
And my drinking cups stopped smelling like perfumes without
preservatives
It started even before you'd given me any
the day you said you wanted me, there was this little helicopter seed on
the ground
I thought I'd save it till it was a memory I could show you
I always felt bad because I didn't give you nearly as many as you gave
me, like I had something to make up for
I did give you a few, though
maybe you remember
that Sunday? When you thought I was gone
You'd run out of space on the countertop
so you threw them away
-
I used to look at them—the ones I kept
Dying
I used to want to crush up the little petals and breathe them
Smoke them

Let the thorns punch holes in my throat when you weren't there
(often)

ALICE has made her way to the flowers. She takes out a matchbox

When you left, I used my glasses for water.
Thank you.
I don't love you.
I hope you're okay.

ALICE strikes the match.

END OF PLAY

MATTHEW WEAVER is a Spokane, Wash., playwright, screenwriter, novelist, and poet. He has multiple full-length plays on the New Play Exchange. He has been produced in 27 states, Canada, Ireland, Japan, and England.

His short penguin drama *Continents Apart* is included in Lawrence Harbison's Best Ten-Minute Plays 2020 anthology. His short play *Willy's Mom Gets in the Car* is included in the Smith & Kraus 2021 Best Ten-Minute Plays anthology.

Short plays include *A New Play by Matthew Weaver*, *Another Play by Matthew Weaver*, *Help! I'm Trapped in a Monologue Written by Matthew Weaver!*, and *19 Excellent Reasons to Date Matthew Weaver*.

Matthew Weaver

4 Horses of the Apocalypse

CHARACTERS:

PALE HORSE   Death's horse

RED HORSE   War's horse

WHITE HORSE   Pestilence's horse

BLACK HORSE   Famine's horse

DEATH   Little girl, aged 6–10

SETTING:

A pasture

NOTES:

First published in the Vassar Review in May 2020, literary arts journal at Vassar College in Poughkeepsie, NY.

Produced for Mystic Vision Players' Kicking & Swearing Festival in Rahway, NJ, in January–February 2020. Directed by Bobby Devarona.

Produced as part of Playwrights Playground, Stage Left Theatre, Spokane, WA, August 2020. Directed by Rebecca Cook.

Sounds of HORSES WHINNYING.

Lights up.

We are in a pasture.

There are four HORSES in the pasture.

They are WHITE HORSE, belonging to Pestilence; BLACK HORSE, belonging to Famine; RED HORSE, belonging to War and PALE HORSE, belonging to Death.

There are four horsemen of the apocalypse, and these are their horses.

WHITE HORSE: (*coughing*)

RED HORSE: Do you think it will be today?

PALE HORSE: Not today.

BLACK HORSE: Good. I'm starving.

RED HORSE: Why not?

WHITE HORSE: (*coughing*) There's really no rush.

RED HORSE: Says you.

BLACK HORSE moves away from WHITE HORSE.

BLACK HORSE: Sick again?

WHITE HORSE: No, no.

RED HORSE: Sick still . . .

BLACK HORSE: Every time you catch something, then I catch it.

WHITE HORSE: Allergies, just allergies. (*sneezes*) Lot of pollen in the air.

PALE HORSE: (*sniffs, contented*) Mmmmm.

BLACK HORSE: Uh huh. Right. More like chicken pox. Or maybe the plague.

RED HORSE: Why can't it be today? Today seems as good as any.

PALE HORSE: Because today . . .

Enter a LITTLE GIRL, 6–10, wearing an adorable outfit, dressed for farm life. A thousand bonus points if the outfit has pockets, is coveralls or she has pigtails.

She has a SKULL for a face.

This is DEATH.

DEATH is never anything more than a little girl—with a skull for a face—who loves and adores horses, for whom horses are the best thing in the whole entire world.

She also carries in her hands a BASKET OF APPLES.

PALE HORSE: . . . there are apples.

The HORSES are excited to see her.

BLACK HORSE: It's food, it's food, it's food! Yay, it's food!

They cluster around DEATH, who giggles and laughs and gently chides and whispers to them.

At some point, DEATH brushes the HORSES. PALE HORSE is her favorite, and she saves RED HORSE for last, as indicated later in the script. Perhaps because RED HORSE is the most temperamental.

The HORSES eat their apples.

WHITE HORSE eats, starts coughing.

PALE HORSE: Slow down. Little bites. Take your time.

WHITE HORSE: I get excited.

Pause.

RED HORSE: If I have to stay in this pasture one more day I'll go mad.

PALE HORSE: (*always gently*) So go mad.
Kick down the fence.
Burn down the barn.
We'll sleep beneath the stars.

WHITE HORSE: (*moaning*) No, no, I'll catch my death.

PALE HORSE: Do not worry friend.
(*indicating DEATH*) She will not let anything happen to us. And besides, the red horse doesn't mean it.

RED HORSE: I don't, do I?! I mean every word. Who are you to say what I do and do not mean?!

PALE HORSE: Sorry, friend. I did not mean to offend. I only observe that every day you fear you will be driven mad . . .

RED HORSE: And so?

PALE HORSE: And every day you are not. I find that comforting.

RED HORSE: I just want it to happen.

PALE HORSE: (*pats the earth with a hoof*) Do not give up on her just yet. There is life in her still.

RED HORSE: Tarnation.

PALE HORSE: Race the black horse around the pasture. That will cheer you up.

BLACK HORSE: Oh no. Oh no. Oh no. I will not race. I'm too hungry to race.

PALE HORSE: I do believe she spilled some clover out of her pockets on the far end.

> *BLACK HORSE is instantly interested.*
>
> *Even though BLACK HORSE is well aware PALE HORSE is lying.*
>
> *RED HORSE prepares to race.*
>
> *This is all a familiar routine.*

BLACK HORSE: . . . I know what you are doing.
It will not work.
(*pause*)
(*It totally is working*) Shut up.

PALE HORSE: And they're off!

> *BLACK HORSE and RED HORSE race offstage.*

WHITE HORSE: (*coughing*) Works every time.

PALE HORSE: One day, it may not work. But we give thanks that it did today.

> *Behind them, BLACK HORSE and RED HORSE run past, still racing.*

WHITE HORSE: (*coughing jag*)

PALE HORSE: That cough becomes worrisome.

WHITE HORSE: Allergies, just allergies.

> *Sounds of a VEHICLE APPROACHING.*
>
> *BLACK HORSE and RED HORSE come flying in.*

BLACK HORSE: I win, I win, I win.

RED HORSE: Is it them?

PALE HORSE: No, no—just someone who went the wrong way. See, they're turning around.

> *Sounds of the VEHICLE departing.*

RED HORSE: Oh.

BLACK HORSE: (*to PALE HORSE, affectionately*) I hate you.

PALE HORSE: (*bemused*) I could have sworn it was clover she dropped. My mistake. And we live to see another day.

RED HORSE: I am not meant to stand around.
I am meant for war.
For slaughter.
To taste blood and spit fire.
To take peace from the earth.

> *PALE HORSE gently nudges an APPLE to the RED HORSE.*

RED HORSE: Thank you.

PALE HORSE: Any moment now.

WHITE HORSE: Any moment?

> *PALE HORSE shakes head.*
>
> *WHITE HORSE relaxes.*
>
> *RED HORSE notices.*

RED HORSE: Don't speak to me as though I am a yearling.

PALE HORSE: My humblest apologies. I spoke in jest under the burden of my affection for existence.

RED HORSE: (*muttering*) When our riders come, when our riders come . . . When we ride . . .

PALE HORSE: If we ride.

> *Pause.*

BLACK HORSE: We can do that?

WHITE HORSE: Our riders, we must obey.

PALE HORSE: I am not so sure it will be a command. I hope it will be a request.

RED HORSE: You would say no? You would turn your back on our duty?

BLACK HORSE: Are you going to finish that apple?

> *RED HORSE passes apple to BLACK HORSE.*
>
> *PALE HORSE nuzzles DEATH, who laughs with glee.*

PALE HORSE: I do not think I could deny this one a thing. All the same, I prefer the illusion of choice.

RED HORSE: There is none.

PALE HORSE: Probably not. And yet it comforts me so. We have oats and clover.

BLACK HORSE: Clover!

PALE HORSE: And apples.
Would be a shame to miss all that.

BLACK HORSE: I want more.

RED HORSE: I want less.

WHITE HORSE: I just want to breathe through my nose.

PALE HORSE: And I am content. Right now. As is.

RED HORSE: Then you are a fool.

> *RED HORSE steps away, angry.*
>
> *But RED HORSE does not go too far, does not leave the stage.*

PALE HORSE: Maybe so, maybe so.

> *RED HORSE paces, furiously muttering.*

BLACK HORSE: Maybe it will be today.

PALE HORSE: Oh, that would make me so sad.
But for her, I would do it. I would do anything.

WHITE HORSE: The red horse may be right . . . it may be exciting.

PALE HORSE: For you three, it would be very exciting.
For we, my rider and I . . .
Our load becomes very heavy.

WHITE HORSE: Alpha and omega.

PALE HORSE: Yes.

BLACK HORSE: The woman and the dragon.

PALE HORSE: Indeed.

BLACK HORSE: It will be a sight to behold.

PALE HORSE: All the more reason to wait.

> *RED HORSE returns.*

RED HORSE: I'm sorry I called you a fool.

PALE HORSE: Not at all, not at all.

RED HORSE: Maybe I am the fool.

PALE HORSE: No.
    Never.
    Not once.

RED HORSE: I just get so mad sometimes.

PALE HORSE: I know.
    Forgiven.
    Forgotten.
    Truly.
    Have another apple.

RED HORSE: I do believe I will.

        RED HORSE eats.

BLACK HORSE: How long have we waited?

WHITE HORSE: Since the—
    (*coughing fit*)
    Since the dawn of time.

RED HORSE: That's a long time to wait for nothing to happen.

        DEATH begins to brush RED HORSE.

        She reaches in her pockets to pull out . . .

DEATH: Sugar cubes!

        Pause.

RED HORSE: . . .
    I suppose it can wait until tomorrow.

PALE HORSE: Deal.

        RED HORSE luxuriates in the sugar and the brushing as we reach . . .

        End of Play

KY WEEKS (they/them) is an actor, author, and playwright currently located in Bellingham, WA. They are a founding member of the Unsubdued Theatre Collective, a democratic artistic group dedicated to creating a revolutionary theatre through collaborative and nonhierarchical means.

Ky Weeks

Crescent Moon Circus

CHARACTERS:

MINS   A young person. They're shy, but trying
                    to work on it.

SLIP   A spiritlike creature. Invisible to most.

SLITHER   A spiritlike creature. Invisible to most.

THE KEEPER   A being of mysterious origins, who seems
                    to be running the show. Wears a mask.

FRIENDS   The friend group that Mins is a part of.
                    (voices only. Can be played by the same actors
                    as Slip, Slither, and the Keeper.)

SETTING:

A mostly empty hotel in a city like any other. Night. Bits of circus
equipment are scattered about the space.

Two monstrous figures (SLIP and SLITHER) enter from unexpected places and scurry across the stage, coming to a stop almost out of sight. Lights up on the window. Everything else is in shadow. MINS stands behind the window, holding a flask, staring inside. Voices of MINS's friends are heard from offstage as they recall the memory of a previous conversation.

FRIEND A: There's a light on in the Crescent Hotel.

FRIEND B: Where?

FRIEND A: Y'know. That place. That hotel. You know.

FRIEND B: Nah, man. Nah. You're wrong. It's under construction. No lights.

FRIEND A: It's been under construction forever.

FRIEND C: No it's not, stupid. It's only under construction if someone's still constructing it. You ever see anyone go in? No.

FRIEND B: Yeah, what I heard was they shut it down a while back. Company ran out of money right before they finished, or everyone died or something. That's why it's empty.

MINS: Except whoever turned the lights on.

FRIEND B: Shut up Mins, the lights aren't on.

FRIEND C: They're on sometimes. I've seen 'em. Some nights they go on.

FRIEND A: That's what I'm saying, man! And if someone goes inside when the lights are on, then they don't ever come out if they don't leave before the sun comes out, right? And if you go in before the lights come on . . .

FRIEND B: Dude, no one cares.

FRIEND A: Yeah, I know. I'm just saying . . .

FRIEND C: Someone should just go in and check it out so we can stop talking about this.

FRIEND A: Not me. Sounds boring.

MINS: Icanmaybecheckitoutiguess.

FRIEND C: What?

FRIEND A: Mins volunteered!

MINS: If it's really so important . . .

FRIEND B: We all heard you Mins! Alright, you'll go in and then come out and tell us whatever you found.

FRIEND A: Maybe you'll find a dead body!

ALL FRIENDS: Mins! Mins! Mins!

MINS waves their hand, silencing the voices. Takes a breath. Holds the flask to their lips.

MINS: For courage.

MINS drinks. Drops the flask. Climbs in through the window. The second they cross, lights up on the whole space, revealing the KEEPER, holding a front desk bell. This startles MINS.

MINS: AAAH! Uh. Hi. I was just. I was coming in, to, uh . . . this isn't where I'm supposed to be. But I'm here. I'm here now. (*The KEEPER presents the bell to MINS*) Thanks, but no. Not for me. (*The KEEPER urgently wants MINS to touch the bell.*) No. Why? What does it do? No.

The KEEPER offers the bell pleadingly. MINS holds out their hand, hesitates over it. The KEEPER gently takes MINS's hand and presses it on the bell. It rings.

KEEPER: Welcome! Thank you for joining us.

MINS: Um, you're welcome I guess? Look, if you were expecting me, I'm not the right person. Whoever that is.

KEEPER: Don't worry. We hear you. There's a place for every dream. You've arrived at the same time that you're here, which is just the right time. You have been heard, and they are coming.

MINS: I don't know what this is. What do you want me to do?

The KEEPER takes a small wrapped chocolate from their pocket and hands it to MINS.

KEEPER: On behalf of all of us, please accept this complementary mint chocolate. You will definitely not want to eat it.

MINS: 'kay.

KEEPER: Everything is ready, so make yourself at home. They have heard you and they will be here soon.

MINS: Should I sit somewhere, or . . .

KEEPER: Unfortunately, due to our time away, some places have experienced slight flooding and decay, and are forever out of order. We take no responsibility. Please forget them. They have heard you and they are coming.

MINS: What do I do when they get here?

KEEPER: Please be quiet. They're here.

MINS: Who?

> SLIP and SLITHER enter from opposite sides, on the ground at first, but crawling/sliding towards each other. They circle one another, trying to stand, but keep fumbling and rolling in an increasingly impressive manner. It's a whole deal. MINS cannot see them.

MINS: Is someone supposed to be here, or . . .

> SLITHER holds up a hoop for SLIP to jump through. SLIP gears up to jump, and then crawls under it. They do a pose.

MINS: I'm waiting? It looks like you're staring at an empty room.

> This dismays SLIP and SLITHER. They put on hats. SLITHER clutches chest and falls, pretending to be dying. SLIP reacts with silent passion, cradling SLITHER, cursing the heavens. Flowers explode from SLITHER, who dies dramatically. SLIP, still silently, writhes in rage and anguish, and dies even more dramatically. Then they both get up and take a bow. KEEPER claps politely. MINS still does not perceive them.

KEEPER: Now then.

MINS: Now what? What were you looking at? Are they here yet?

KEEPER: Don't worry, that's how the show looks to everyone at first. But there's no time to think about that, it's your cue. Time to go on.

MINS: Hold up. Whatever you want me to do, I can't.

KEEPER: The lights are on for you.

MINS: No. Sorry. Sorry, no.

KEEPER: No? So then why are you with us today?

MINS: Because. No reason. No one cares, right? It's better than being in my room. Better than the nightmares when I sleep. That's all. That's the only reason.

KEEPER: Take your time. We're all here. Everyone is here. It's always now.

> MINS unwraps the mint chocolate.

MINS: For courage.

KEEPER: For courage.

> MINS eats the chocolate. As soon as they do, they are able to perceive SLIP and SLITHER. This is mildly disturbing.

SLIP and SLITHER: Welcome back.

They push MINS forwards, as strange, lively music (think **Danse Macabre***) begins to play. KEEPER watches with anticipation. SLIP offers MINS a juggling club. MINS takes it, examines it, spins it, tosses it in the air, gets familiar with it. SLITHER tosses two more, which MINS catches easily and breaks into a full routine, juggling, dancing, exploring possibilities of movement. Much spinning is done. SLIP and SLITHER continue to hand MINS more materials, hoops, ribbons, etc. which are seamlessly incorporated into the performance. SLIP and SLITHER react with great joy and rapture, fully joining in the festivities, flipping and moving around MINS as they get increasingly lost in the show. The performance rises in intensity, and then suddenly stops. MINS drops what they were holding, amazed at what has just happened. MINS is fully one of them.*

Blackout. End of play.

MICHAEL YICHAO is a playwright, actor, and game designer currently residing in Seattle, WA. His plays have received recognition from the O'Neill Theater's National Playwright's Conference (Finalist, *jellyfish pine*) and the John F Kennedy Performing Arts Center (KCACTF winner 2011–2013), among others. Yichao has been an invited playwright at the Last Frontier Theater Conference, Great Plains Theater Conference, and the Association of Theater in Higher Education (ATHE) Conference.

In addition to his theatrical work, Yichao has served as a narrative and creative lead for video games and themed entertainment. Past work includes Disney Imagineering, ArenaNet, Riot Games, Wizards of the Coast, and Phoenix Labs. He currently is co-founder and Chief Creative Officer at Jam & Tea Studios, a new game company. @michaelyichao | Michaelyichao.com

Michael Yichao

Bread

CHARACTERS:

olivia

dan

SETTING:

high school lunchtime. a lunch table, outdoors.

dan and olivia. juniors. olivia tries to read a book of poems.
dan eats a sandwich.

olivia: i hate this

dan: it's just poetry

olivia: it's stupid
  pointless
  makes no sense

dan: just read the book

  she does. for like, five seconds.

olivia: why can't they just say what they mean
  instead of all this metaphor
  simile
  bullshit

dan: you hate all poetry?

olivia: "you are the bread and the knife
  the crystal goblet and the wine"
  blah blah blah

dan: "you are the dew on the grass
  and the burning wheel of the sun"

olivia: . . . you have this memorized

dan: that one's my favorite

olivia: it doesn't even rhyme

dan: it's poetry
  not hallmark cards

olivia: it's dumb is what it is

dan: you're dumb

olivia: your face

dan: your mom

  a swat with the book.
  an instinctual block with the sandwich.
  a stuck out tongue.
  an eye roll.
  a beat.
  a bite.
  a moment of reading.

olivia: i haaaaaate this

dan: you hate everything today

olivia: just this
and ms kline
(that bitch)

dan: whoa, hey! But she's so nice!

olivia: boning all the football players

dan: rumors

olivia: you just like her cuz she liked your dead puppy poem

dan: . . . maybe
(*laughs*) but she hated melinda's dead grandma poem
oh man that was harsh

olivia: see? Bitch

dan: no, not her fault
a dying dog is tragic
grandmas are just . . . too real

olivia: . . . that's messed up

dan: well, i like her
and poetry

olivia: you're the only one
nerd

dan: kevin wrote a good poem

olivia: kevin's asian
overachiever genes
doesn't actually like this crap

dan: he's asian?

olivia: um, yes? half i think
so half an overachiever
(just an achiever?)

dan: it's just
piercing blue eyes . . .

olivia: oh
oh man

dan: . . . no—it's not like that—

olivia: you totally wanna bone him

dan: i don't—trust me—gross—

olivia: gross? cuz he's half asian?
   racist

dan: you're putting words

olivia: in your mouth

dan: stop

olivia: where you want kevin's—

dan: you're so freaking crass

olivia: what, because i'm a girl?
   girls can't talk like that?

dan: no, it's just

olivia: misogynist
   (and racist)

dan: i'm not—
   i love girls

olivia: and boys

dan: . . . i'm never telling you anything ever again

olivia: until the next time we drink
   or play truth or dare
   or sit around in my room staring at the walls
   (like we do every tuesday after your stupid soccer practice)

dan: i hate you

olivia: hey! come on
   when did you get so sensitive

dan: i'm not

olivia: just a little teasing

dan: it's just
   a sensitive thing

olivia: that's what she said
   or he said, rather

dan: shut up! Jeeze

olivia: i should go tell kevin you—

dan: don't!
   don't

       dammit, livi, just
       leave it alone

           headdesk. a lull. genuine concern.

olivia: . . . hey
       i was just kidding
       you know that, right?

dan: you haven't told anyone—

olivia: no!
       of course not
       but
       i didn't realize it was a secret
       . . . i mean
       it's pretty obvious

dan: what

olivia: well
       uh
       you're into theater
       and choir
       and you have an impeccable sense of fashion

dan: stereotyping, nice
       what about soccer

olivia: gayest of all sports!
       and you wear scarves
       scarves
       and you know how to tie a bow tie

dan: that doesn't make me gay
       i just like boys
       (some of the time)

olivia: part time gay?

dan: i dunno
       those words
       gay
       bi
       just sound weird when i use them on me

olivia: danny boy:
       defies all the categories
       no one can box daniel in

dan: please don't be patronizing—
   you know what
   you're right
   i'm just being oversensitive
   i dunno why i'm freaking out

olivia: hey
   you're not oversensitive
   just
   sensitive
   it's not a bad thing
   girls dig that
   (boys too?)

dan: feels weird still
   you're the first i told, so hearing you say it out loud—

olivia: i'm the first?

dan: of course
   who else would i tell?

olivia: sorry
   oh wow, sorry
   usually i'm much more aware

dan: usually you're a mind reader
   just cuz you're not for a minute today
   doesn't mean anything
   it's probably cuz you already knew
   that i'm . . .
   so you didn't know it would matter
   to say it out loud
   but it does
   (a little)

olivia: i don't read minds
   i just know yours too well
   with its interesting curves and squishy bits

dan: . . . thanks

olivia: you're the only one i can mind read
   you're special

dan: a little snowflake

olivia: no
   you are not the snowflake

you are . . . the bread and the knife
you're not the, the last beam of sunset
that rare flash of green before vanishing beneath
an infinite horizon
just the bread
and
the
knife

she's gotten close. he breathes in.

dan: i hate you

olivia: you are the bread and the knife
i am just the cafeteria pizza

dan: hey, pizza's good
i love pizza

olivia: i love your mom

dan: i love your mom's face

olivia: your face's mom

dan: your face's . . . face

olivia: (*laughing*) what?

dan: i love your face

olivia: . . . what?

dan suddenly kisses olivia.
surprise.
she doesn't kiss him back.
he pulls away.
awkward moment.
REALLY awkward moment.

dan: uh
sorry
shit

olivia: . . . you are the stupidest boy i've ever met

dan: sorry
i'm sorry
i
sorry

olivia: stop saying sorry

dan: sorry

olivia: . . .

dan: . . . sorry

olivia: ARGH!
    you're a caveman
    sorry sorry sorry
    a one word caveman

dan: i'm a caveman
    because i have no words for you
    to fill you
    to take your shape, trace your outline
    your being

olivia: poetic

dan: no you are

olivia: no you are

dan: no your face is

olivia: your mom is
    in bed

      a bit of silence.

olivia: why tell me you like boys
    then kiss me

dan: that is the question, huh

olivia: do you even like boys?

dan: yes!
    i mean
    yes
    i guess it was easier telling you the first secret
    than the second

olivia: . . . are you trying to say i look like a boy?

dan: no
    what
    you know that's not
    i hate you

olivia: you hate everything today

dan: yeah, well

olivia: you make no sense

dan: i know

olivia: you're a poem that doesn't rhyme

dan: it's easier being a hallmark card

> *beat. in the distance, a school bell rings.*
> *the two continue to sit.*

dan: i think i'd like to kiss you again—

olivia: no

dan: okay that's fine
  . . . maybe later?

olivia: you're dumb

dan: yeah

> *olivia throws her book in her backpack, stands to leave.*
> *dan sits, staring into space.*

olivia: . . . maybe later

> *olivia walks away.*
> *dan watches her walk off, surprised.*
> *smiles.*

dan: you are my bread and the knife.

APPENDIX: PRODUCTION & CONTACT INFORMATION

For all rights, including amateur and student performances, please contact the playwrights directly with the information provided.

JOIE DE VIVRE by Suzanne Bailie had its first production at Olympic Theater Arts Center New Works Showcase, June 16–18, 2021, directed by Christy Holy.
CONTACT: suzibailie@yahoo.com

DADDY by Kelleen Conway Blanchard had its first production at 14/48: The World's Quickest Theater Festival at Consolidated Works (ConWorks), January 10, 2004, directed by Tom Milewski, performed by Peggy Gannon, Jen Moon, Troy Lund, Mark Boeker, and Jennifer Jasper.
CONTACT: https://newplayexchange.org/users/780/kelleen-conway-blanchard

I'M SORRY ABOUT THE RAW EGGS I HID IN YOUR APARTMENT (AND/THE/TIME/I/TRIMMED/YOUR/HAIR) by Anuhea Brown had its first production at FINDING TRAILS with Penguin Productions, October 2020, directed by Agastya Kohli, performed by Esha More (RHEA) and Samir Shah (JOHN).
CONTACT: www.anuheaisbrown.com, anuheabrown1@gmail.com

I'M AFRAID OF SLEEP (OR WAKING UP), WILL YOU STAY WITH ME BEFORE I FALL? by Brian Dang had its first production at *RESILIENCE!: An AAPI 24-Hour Play Festival* on Zoom with Pork Filled Productions, November 2021, directed by Kiefer Harrington, performed by Fune Tautala.
CONTACT: www.brianeatswords.com

CAPSULE by Bret Fetzer had its first production at 14/48: The World's Quickest Theater Festival at Consolidated Works, July 2002, directed by Christina Mastin, performed by Jon Milazzo, Sarah Shipley, Eric Starker, and Jonah von Spreecken.
CONTACT: bret.fetzer@annextheatre.org.

THERE'S A WORD FOR THAT by Mikki Gillette had its first reading at Fuse Theatre Ensemble, April 2022, directed by Asae Dean, performed by Ruby Welch (Poe) and Kyron McCoy (Eddie).
CONTACT: mikkigillette.com; mikkigillette@gmail.com

SAFE by Ki Gottberg had its first production at 14/48: The World's Quickest Theater Festival in Seattle, 2011.
CONTACT: ki@seattleu.edu

LITTLE MOONS by Emily Haver had its first production at One World Theatre (Shanghai, China), June 2018, directed by De Anne Dubin, performed by Astrid Larrea (YOUNG WOMAN) and James Robert Lyon (YOUNG MAN).
CONTACT: www.emilyhaver.com, emhaver@gmail.com

LIVING DONOR by Maggie Lee had its first production at 14/48: The World's Quickest Theater Festival at ACT Theatre (Seattle, WA), January 2018, directed by Wesley Frugé, performed by Ana María Campoy, Hannah Mootz, André Nelson, and Evan Whitfield.
CONTACT: maggie.lee.playwright@gmail.com

HOLY HELL by Barbara Lindsay had its first production at the Five and Dime Playwriting Contest with CrossCurrent Culture (Kansas City, MO), August 2002, directed by Judy Clause, performed by Tyler Miller (The Man) and Lesli Crawford (The Woman).
CONTACT: barbaralindsayplaywright.com, babzella@babzella.com, (206) 214-6664

BE BATMAN by Willow McLaughlin had its first production at Anacortes Community Theatre, July 2019, directed by Willow McLaughlin, performed by Heather DeGroot (MAY) and Abigail Hanson (LEA).
CONTACT: willow.mclaughlin@gmail.com, (360) 395-8107

THIRTY STORY MASTERPIECES by July Monday had its first production at Red Fern (NYC), March 2009.
CONTACT: 13chairs@gmail.com. 13 Chairs is an organization that supports writers with mental illnesses. https://fundraising.fracturedatlas.org/13-chairs

JOSH'S REAL FUNERAL by Beth Raas-Bergquist had its first production at 14/48: The World's Quickest Theater Festival, January 2016, directed by Neil Redding.
CONTACT: bethraas@gmail.com, (206) 852-6743

THE SCARY QUESTION by Wayne Rawley had its first production at Annex Theatre in Seattle, WA, February 6, 2004, performed by Shannon Kipp (LINDA) and Wayne Rawley (BRIAN).
CONTACT: Playscripts, Inc. through playscripts.com

DOCTOR LOOPIFER'S MACHINE by Matt Smith had its first production at The Phoenix Theatre in collaboration with Tim Noah Thumbnail Theater, August 2019, directed by Eric Lewis, performed by Chelsea Burlile, Stacy Lynn Gilbert, and Melanie Calderwood.
CONTACT: www.mattwritesplays.com

DON'T FEED DEAD ROSES YOUR DRINKING WATER by Ozzy Wagner had its first reading at the Kennedy Center American College Theater Festival, 2021.
CONTACT: ozzyrwagner@gmail.com, bit.ly/ozzynpx

4 HORSES OF THE APOCALYPSE by Matthew Weaver had its first production at the Kicking & Swearing Festival, Mystic Vision Players (Rahway, NJ), January–February 2020, directed by Bobby Devarona, performed by Karen Carratura (Red Horse), Jason Muldowney (Pale Horse), Serena Marie Williams (White Horse), Ty'zhe Boyd (Black Horse), and Lorelle Lane (Death).
CONTACT: newplayexchange.org/users/9069/matthew-weaver, WeaverRMatthew@gmail.com

CRESCENT MOON CIRCUS by Ky Weeks had its first production at Sylvia Center for the Arts, September 2021, directed by Bradley M(dot) Dillon, performed by Nika Roberts (Mins), Clare Koesters (The Keeper), Jason Stach (Slip), and Bradley M(dot) Dillon (Slither).
CONTACT: kyweekswrites@gmail.com

BREAD by Michael Yichao had its first production as the recipient of the Kennedy Center Gary Garrison National Ten Minute Play Award, 2014.
CONTACT: michaelyichao.com

A. REY PAMATMAT

A. Rey Pamatmat's plays include *Edith Can Shoot Things and Hit Them* (Actors Theatre of Louisville), *after all the terrible things I do* (Milwaukee Rep), *House Rules* (Ma-Yi), *Thunder Above, Deeps Below* (Second Generation), *A Spare Me* (Waterwell), and *DEVIANT*. His newest play, *Safe, Three Queer Plays*, follows the seismic changes in Queer America through a gay man of color's life. Rey also recently contributed to a collaborative libretto for *Desert In*, which premiered on the Boston Lyric Opera's operabox.tv. His work has been translated into Spanish and Russian, performed in Mexico, Puerto Rico, and Russia, and published by Concord Theatricals, Playscripts, Cambria Press, and Vintage. Rey is the former co-director of the Ma-Yi Writers Lab, and was a PoNY, Hodder, and Princess Grace Fellow.

RAIN CITY PROJECTS was founded by Mark Lutwak. Previous board members include Steve Alter, Nikki Appino, Meghan Arnette, Scot Augustson, Lenore Bensinger, Becky Bruhn, Susanna Burney, Morgain Cole, Andrew Lee Creech, Drew Emery, Warren Etheredge, Adam Greenfield, Wier Harmon, John Holyoke, Andy Jensen, Brendan Kiley, Robin Kilrain, Darian Lindle, Tod McCoy, S. P. Miskowski, Paul Mullin, Allison Narver, K. Brian Neel, Madeleine Oldham, Olga Sanchez, Matt Smith, Meg Stevenson, Kristina Sutherland Rowell, Sean Ryan, Stephanie Timm, Montana Von Fliss, and Y York.

CURRENT BOARD OF DIRECTORS are Anuhea Brown, Kate Danley, Monika Elmont, Maggie Lee, and Juliet Waller.

Made in United States
Troutdale, OR
02/20/2024

17829185R00096